Thailand Transplant Tales
and
How to Become a Gentleman Farmer in Thailand

by Gordon Bennett

GW00730575

Copyright © 2016 Gordon Bennett

All rights reserved, including the right to reproduce this book, or portions thereof in any form. No part of this text may be reproduced, transmitted, downloaded, decompiled, reverse engineered, or stored, in any form or introduced into any information storage and retrieval system, in any form or by any means, whether electronic or mechanical without the express written permission of the author.

ISBN: 978-1-326-53767-8

PublishNation
www.publishnation.co.uk

Introduction

I sold my business in Western country in 2011and retired at age 63. After about 2 years of retirement, for a variety of reasons explained in the book, my Thai wife of eight years and I, decided to go and live in Thailand. She owned a property that included a fruit farm that had been neglected of proper maintenance or development for eight years while we were living together overseas and she now had purchased her family home since her father died. This house also would need some maintenance and a degree of modernisation to make it comfortable for our use while we enjoy a few years early in my retirement, living in the sun & doing some travelling.

Looking back on the first almost two years spent actually living in Thailand, as I re-read this introduction, I suddenly grasped the magnitude of what we have achieved in under two years. We have remodelled most of a 35 year old farm house into a comfortable modern home for Thai or Western residents. We have also built from scratch two more houses, one, a fairly basic place (hopefully) for farm workers to live in and one very comfortable, cool, thoroughly modern Thai country family home with three bedrooms and two bathrooms. The reasons and circumstances for building this house are explained in the book but it was not intended as an immediate home for us. In fact it was not intended to be built at all!

In addition we have re-developed the two hectare (five acre) orchard that has had minimal money or maintenance spent on in for at least the last five years. The pruning, fertilizing and irrigation upgrades have been a very big job, with no onsite staff and occasional "blitzes" from gangs of relatively unskilled migrant workers who usually only plant or harvest Cassava (also known as Manioc or Arrowroot.)

Most of the farm work has been done with only the help from various family members, paid and unpaid, plus the contract spraying and the migrant worker blitzes. The effort and expenditure has been

1

worth it because the crops should be much bigger this year and increase every year for the next 3-5 years.

So why have I written this book; and why would anyone want to read about my life anyway?

Well, Thailand is an interesting place that many people seem to be eternally curious about it. I have been told by several friends, that by many peoples' standards I am actually "living the life" whatever that means; and that people **would** be interested in my experiences. We'll see!

It was not like writing from scratch because much of the groundwork was done already. I am one of these people who finds that by putting my thoughts down on paper, it actually clarifies my thinking and helps me make (I hope) better decisions. Also, because I may not decide to stay here for the rest of my natural life, I have been writing newsletters to keep in touch with friends & family back home. Quite long newsletters, actually, and they, edited & added to, form the backbone for this book. I guess this is where they got the idea that we were living some exotic romantic adventure.

So the other reason for the newsletters is that, I have had several friends move overseas for one reason or another and never heard from them again. Since I moved, several of my formerly very close friends hardly contact me at all. So, if I decide for some reason to move "back home" again in the future, I want my old friends to remember who I was. So I take the initiative and send regular email newsletter updates.

So, aren't there enough books on advice already for foreigners contemplating moving here?

Well yes, but most foreigners (Farangs) only visit tourist areas and go by public transport or tours through the country. For cultural reasons, decent Thai women are difficult to meet. Most decent Thai women are nervous of being seen even by family, in the company of a Farang, as it raises questions about their own morality. (Read: Is she a part-time prostitute?) For this reason, most advice books cover the subject of prostitution and the problems of relationships with bar girls and the common problems of their bad habits with money, possessions, drugs, alcohol, fidelity and gambling. So male tourists tend to meet lots of "good time girls" but have relatively few opportunities to meet eligible decent Thai women with good attitudes to relationships, home & family. Even women they meet innocently in a holiday or tourist situation are used to being lied to & emotionally cheated by tourists' empty promises, so have learned to act in the same manner. And then there are the gamblers, hard-luck-story purveyors, not to mention the liars who still have the husband that they claim is an ex-husband. Or a boyfriend/pimp that she gives all her money to!!

Many tourist town girls become addicted to the bar/tourist/easy money/party lifestyle and cannot (or will not) even admit it to themselves. These books all tell you how **"you can take the girl out of the bar but you can't take the bar out of the girl."**

I will assume you have read at least two or three of these books already. If you have not, you need to do it immediately or you run the risk of making all the classic tourist mistakes, falling in love/lust within your first 24 hours and being dragged into a gold shop on your third day. Don't laugh. It happens!

So, what audience am I writing for?

Most "how to" or "why not to" books involve living in a condo in Pattaya, Phuket or Chiang Mai etc with one (or a series) of local partners. Many of them are obviously written by people with profitable investments back home or sufficient funds to not need another income in Thailand. A number of them discuss village life in a more remote part of the kingdom but not many, talk about the things I needed to know about. Other books rarely include any advice on farming or farm business management to help a foreign husband understand the challenges ahead. He and his Thai wife will need help on a number of topics to create an income from her land, improve their standard of living and reduce the demand on funds or assets based overseas. Such as: Employing builders. Water, wells, suitable crops, spraying, home security, dog ownership, poisonous insects and reptiles, burglary, theft & con-tricks. Even just dealing with shopkeepers can be a mission when you are the only Farang in or near that town.

This book assumes you have got past most of the usual areas of advice covered in other books

You have either met, or intend to try and meet that golden nugget; **a decent Thai woman with a good attitude to relationships,** as mentioned above. You may even be married to a good Thai woman, approaching your retirement age and wondering what to do with your life. Or like me, already retired and not happy with your life. She may already have land or you have discussed living in Thailand together to cut down retirement living costs & she either has a farming background or genuinely likes living in the rural setting. (Meaning: She is not going to get bored with the countryside, five minutes after you buy twenty rai of land in her name!)

But almost certainly, you have at most, only a vague idea how to handle all the challenges that we faced. My wife's family includes many farmers but they are all younger than me, acclimatised to the heat away from the cooler coastal weather and used to working seven days with only occasional religious holidays off. Some of their advice was not applicable to us and also, we made mistakes. Sometimes we had to work out a solution that worked for us but was outside the traditional country family way of operating a farm. I do not want my wife out working every day in the heat. And of course, we want a life, to enjoy our time together and fulfil our dream to travel occasionally.

If this sounds a bit like you, or what you would like to do, then you are the person this was written for.

This book is actually two books in one!

This book of roughly 40,000 words is one single volume, eighteen chapters, divided into two parts, helpfully called "Part One" and "Part Two." The two parts have their own series of numbered and named chapters.

Part One is really about the background of how we got here, and the adventures and experiences we have had in the first crazy two years of our "transplant." In its ten chapters I hope to entertain you a little with our adventures, and you are invited to laugh at and learn from our mistakes. I earnestly suggest you do not attempt to experience all our mistakes for yourself.

Part Two is to try and ensure you do NOT make many of the mistakes we made in part one.

It contains information about land, living in the countryside and farming in Thailand. And hopefully, helpful advice based mainly on our own research and experiences. This second part comprises eight chapters and each chapter is laid out with groups of related subjects, headed and titled for easy reference.

One last point regarding my privacy: I have chosen to write under a pen name and not offer details about our exact location or other personal identifying details. This is to protect us from unexpected visitors and to protect the guilty in my narrative as well as the innocent. I have provided an email address at the end of the book. I have a busy life here and we are currently trying to catch up on the travel we promised ourselves and have not got round to yet. I will check my email regularly and try to answer honestly any reasonable questions arising from this book that I consider are within my areas of expertise and not too longwinded or complicated. Do not expect the answer next day, but it might happen, you never know. I hope you enjoy our adventures and experiences.

Part One: Transplant Tales

Chapter 1

The background...
and how it all got started

"Darling, don't give me an answer now, but my idea is this: What say we go and live at my home in Thailand for a few years? Mother is eighty-two now and getting really lonely since dad died and misses me terribly. We could upgrade the house there to make it comfortable for us to live in and build up the orchard again. If it was making some money and we got in some local staff to help us, we would be able to do the travelling in Vietnam, Myanmar and Laos that we keep promising ourselves. Don't answer now, but will you at least think about it?"

To her surprise, my answer was an immediate "Yes!" as I had privately been thinking the same idea through for several months, but for my own reasons. This conversation happened in May 2013 and at that point I had been officially retired for eighteen months. Unfortunately, I was already finding that things were not turning out exactly the way I had hoped they would in my earlier-than-planned-for retirement.

Historical and geographic background and my family connection with Thailand

South East Asia has always been an interesting place for Western travellers to visit, in an "adventure tourism" sort of way. Of course the term adventure tourism had not been invented in the 1960s but between the early 1960s and the late 1980s it became an extremely interesting place to visit. In fact, for many people, it became a fatally interesting place if you happened to be "in the wrong place at the wrong time", or were just "dead unlucky" to live there or be posted there.

During this time, millions of people died in South East Asia; in political wars, cultural revolutions and ethnic bloodbaths throughout the region. The USA took over the Vietnam War when the French lost interest after Diem Bien Phu. The Burmese military took over Burma/Myanmar, put Aung San Suu Kyi under house arrest and entered decades of ethnic unrest. Pol Pot took over Cambodia to show the Chinese how to really do the "Proletarian Paradise" thing, killing possibly millions in the process. And several countries were trying to either take over Laos, control it as a buffer state, or bomb it back to the stone age.

In the centre of all this geographically, was Thailand, a somewhat fragile democracy since the revolution of 1932, before which it had been an absolute monarchy. And into this interesting region, in 1974, went the younger of my two older sisters with her husband and four young children on a two to three year jaunt to live in Khon Kaen, in North East Thailand.

Khon Kaen is in Isaan territory, whose citizens are physically a combination of lowland Laos and Cambodian stock, culturally Lao and now legally Thai. Laos has its own language and distinctive writing script. Some people may take issue with me saying that Lao is a bit like a simplified version of Thai, but I qualify this by saying that there are many similar words, but some parts of the grammar seem less complicated than Thai, in particular, not having the Thai male/female "Krap" or "Kaa" on the end of every statement.

The collection of Isaan provinces, officially termed "North East Thailand" were previously part of Laos and therefore, also previously part of what was French Indo-China, (Laos, Cambodia and Vietnam) but these territories has been gradually absorbed by Thailand over the last 150 or so years. This was sort of finally settled in an 1893 treaty with France when the Mekong river sensibly became the border at last and settling a major sticking point for Thailand. And settled again, further, by the brief Franco–Thai war of 1940-1941, while France was under German rule and had virtually no credible functioning army in the region. If you have time, it is interesting to read the Wikipedia account of this brief war and the later reversal of some of the territories gained as spoils of this war, a war which many people have either forgotten about, or never even knew it happened.

Certainly my family found Thailand an interesting place to have an overseas adventure in the 1970s, as did hundreds of thousands of American soldiers, sailors and airmen who were either based in Thailand or who took their Rest and recreation (R and R) in Thailand during the Vietnam War, which was waged during this same chaotic era. Possibly with different experiences, though.

My brother-in-law was employed as a civil engineer, supervising design and construction on part of a large international aid project. They were part of building a university, a hospital and a medical school in Khon Kaen. My parents visited them twice at their Thai home in Khon Kaen. They also travelled elsewhere in Thailand and loved the place. My other older sister and her husband also made two trips, but later, after the younger sister and her family had returned home to live, and they all loved Thailand too. Around 1992, I separated from my first wife of twenty years, started another business and took to having a two to four week overseas holiday in February every year. The first time or two, I went to Fiji. After that it was Thailand every year, with side trips into Laos and Cambodia, for the next twelve or so years. (But who's counting?) And I loved Thailand too!

During this time at home I had taken in as a flatmate a Thai speaking Welsh bachelor. He was on a mission to return to Thailand to live, this time as an ex-pat English teacher. Some two years later he moved to Thailand and ended up in a city an hour or two out of Bangkok. I used to visit him and his Thai wife, a university English and teaching graduate, at the end of each of my annual holidays to Thailand. I was travelling on my own of course, but during two or three of these annual visits I met most of his wife's family; parents, grandparents, siblings, cousins, the lot. Eventually, during my 2005 trip I ruined both my bachelor status and my bachelor lifestyle by meeting one of his wife's aunties whom I had previously not met. We fell in love, married a year later in 2006 and she left Thailand to be with me in my home country "to live together, happily ever after".

Of course, if that was all that had happened, then the rest of this book would not exist. But as we all know life frequently does not turn out the way we plan things.

Folk history tells us that the Norse raiders used to burn their boats and leave their women and children on the beach to stiffen their resolve for when they attacked a Scottish or English village. It might make you fight harder but it tends to make things somewhat inconvenient if you lose a battle or decide you are homesick. The significance of this piece of history is that although we moved to Thailand to live, we did not "burn our boats". We still retain options because we currently still own our house back home, so:

(1) We get a handy rental off it which pays nearly all the mortgage.

(2) We have a crash pad to stay in when we pop home for any reason, and

(3) Most importantly, we are still on the real estate ladder back home. If you live in a major metropolitan area in many Western countries, and you sell your house to go overseas for five years or more, you may never be able to afford to buy a house back in the same market again. So, our options are open if we decide after a few years that we don't want to live in Thailand anymore, or if health or any other circumstance intervenes.

I think that if these personal safeguards were not in place for us we would not have made this move so lightly. I urge any person planning a move like this to think the consequences through very carefully. If you are not absolutely certain about the move being permanent, try to hedge your bets by keeping your house and renting it, at least for several years. If you can rent your home either furnished, or store your stuff SECURELY and insured in Auntie Mary's garage, then all is good. If you do not own a home or decide to sell up before you leave home then you had better have a well-researched "Plan B" available to fall back on at semi-immediate notice if things don't work out in Thailand for you.

One other bit of future-proofing I started soon after arriving was sending semi-regular newsletters to the friends and relatives back home. I tried to keep them involved with our doings so they would still remember us if and when we went home, either for visits or to live. You've got to look after those potential free beds and meals! Those newsletters also provided the notes and the time framework for this book.

I had planned to continue working until at least age sixty-five years and perhaps beyond, in a retail business jointly owned by myself and a business partner of the same age. These last few years of peak earnings were going to be really important to top off my retirement fund and help make things a bit more comfortable for us. This was particularly important as I had remarried again and now needed a bigger retirement nest egg for two, than I did as a single person. I thought I had a pretty good plan going until, at age sixty-two, my partner told me he wanted to retire from our business. In other investments for retirement preparedness, he was several years ahead of me, but of course I had a plan to deal with that. A plan that suddenly went "belly up"!

I did not want the financial liability or the responsibilities of the business all on my own so I agreed to sell the business and we eventually completed the sale a bit over a year later in October 2011.

After I remarried in 2006, my new wife came and lived with me in my country for over seven years, the first five of which I was still working. She had settled well in her new country with me and had been in school. She had learned to speak good English and she had made many friends. She was forty years old and had already started two businesses including running an import business, with my assistance, from the basement "rumpus-room" in our home. She was importing a range of niche Thai cultural and Buddhist products unavailable there, which we sold by internet auction, our own website and at Buddhist and Thai holiday fairs to loyal, mostly Thai customers.

By May 2013, at age sixty-five I had already sold my retail business and been retired for eighteen months. I was feeling a little bored and unfulfilled, but mainly I was concerned about the future of my wife's businesses. Her import business was growing nicely but the business model had a few problems which had started to become apparent. She had also gained quite a following as a Thai fortune teller two years before and the import business was really an add on to the fortune telling, which was a "nice little earner" all on its own. Fortune telling required no stock to be held and there were no airfares or international freight to pay and no websites to maintain. But the two income streams had become inter-dependent on each other, while one had considerable overhead costs the other had almost none.

Also, her personal presence had become vital to the success of both businesses. When she was not there the fortune telling income obviously stopped completely, but sales in the import business also slowed to a trickle. The original thinking was to have a Thai friend manage the business when she or we were both away. This began to look impractical because without her the import business would not support the wages of part-time staff, and turnover dropped to a point that did not really warrant me or anyone else being there. And she needed to go away to Thailand for a buying trip for a month or more, two or three times a year. If you add in the retirement holiday travel we wanted to take, then we could have a business that closed several times a year for up to four or six months. Ouch!

We had trained my wife's sisters in Thailand to be really good at packing the orders up securely for shipping, but there was no replacing my wife as the buyer because they did not really understand our market. Therefore, they could only buy and ship certain quite specific products without her being there to do the buying.

Meanwhile, her reputation at our home as a fortune teller had spread beyond the Thai community and this brought its own problems. Tarot card reading for non-Thai customers meant she now had to explain her readings in English, usually to other Asians (Chinese, Cambodian, Indian, Sri Lankan etc). This was a huge strain given the subtleties involved and that English was only a second language to both her and her customers. She wanted to say "No" to non-Thai customers, but saying "No" resulted in unpleasantness and even threats of racial prejudice among other threats from some Asian customers. She was considering stopping that work completely.

We appeared to be building a trap for ourselves with only a part-year income, almost totally reliant on my wife's presence and personality. The business model shortcomings suddenly were very obvious. If she stopped the fortune telling could the import business provide a worthwhile profit margin with all the same overheads and only one quarter of the net income? The answer in my opinion was "NO", so I mapped out in advance the steps necessary to form the profile of my then, "Plan B – Thailand". When she independently suggested the same idea to me, my immediate answer was "Yes," much to her considerable surprise.

I was retired but actually quite busy with the Thai imports website, photographing and editing pictures and adding products. I also had another small business interest too, but even that could not keep me enthused when I could see we were building a trap for ourselves with an income that would be worse than one person working at McDonald's by the time the income was divided by two. The view of the gallows always focuses the mind, so we are told.

Chapter 2

Making the move

So, we started planning the details and she flew to Thailand in August 2013, but not on a buying trip this time. She went to discuss our plans with the family and to try and get builders to start work on the first stage of our home improvement project. We needed to re-roof and close-in the large open kitchen area on the other side of the securely fenced internal home courtyard. Concrete block walls and glass partitions had to be erected, and a plasterboard ceiling with roof ventilation had to be installed. This large area was to be partitioned into two rooms, one with air con as a day room for us and the other as a kitchen/dining room.

While she was in Thailand I converted our upstairs bathroom into a bathroom/laundry. This would let us convert the downstairs rumpus/business area into a semi-independent flat for us as it already had its own bathroom, toilet and a sort of "half kitchen". This would be somewhere we could completely lock off, with its own alarm and security, to store our furniture and give us a crash pad when we came home for any reason. As we now had an upper floor bathroom/laundry, leaks became a risk with the lower floor sealed off so the bathroom floor had to be "tanked up" to the walls and floor drains installed.

My optimistic budget of $4,000 went to $12,000 or $14,000 (but again, who's counting) as we replaced rotten flooring from older leaks in the bathroom and the invoices from electrical and plumbing sub-contractors started mounting up. It was completed, paint and all, before she got back in early September 2013, and she never even knew I was going to do it while she was away.

As I only did what tenants "needed" as opposed to what we "wanted", the decisions I had to make were simpler, but still more expensive than I expected. Fortunately she was delighted with the results when I did the "OK, Honey, now open your eyes," trick, the day she returned. The results of her construction efforts in Thailand are covered in a later chapter.

We announced the "closing-down" sale just before she flew to Thailand in August, and between us we sold or disposed of most of the stock and the fittings downstairs to allow us to move a much reduced furniture house lot down from upstairs. There is almost room for us there too, but we do not have a proper kitchen there. We do have our fridge, some cupboards and a laundry with water supply. While it isn't exactly home, it is a crash pad, and we still have many of our important possessions while we work out our future lives. And we still have our options open which is so important as I have explained, a few paragraphs back.

We were able to rent out our house to someone we knew well and moved to Thailand on the 17th of December 2013. Another Ex-pat or "Farang" as the Thais call us non-Asian-non-Thais, had arrived to live in the L.O.S. (Land of Smiles). But not to live in a condo in Phuket, Pattaya or Chiang Mai. We moved onto my wife's five acre fruit farm about two hours out of Bangkok, and that is what this book is all about.

Chapter 3

The adventure begins

So here we were at Chinese New Year in Thailand in early February 2014 trying to find another builder. The builder who had agreed to come back to work when we returned had asked us to wait until the end of January for him, then after making us waste six weeks changed his mind. I had lost about five kilos in that six weeks, just on my changed diet and daily routines, and I had started on insulating and refurbishing the upstairs of the homestead while waiting for the builder to return.

I should mention, in case you were wondering, that we already owned a vehicle in Thailand for three years. We had purchased a four-door Toyota Hilux VIGO pickup truck with a fibreglass canopy in 2011, when my wife was running back and forth buying stock for her import business.

We live in a rural area, four kilometers from the nearest rural shopping centre and an hour travel in two directions to either of the nearest two big cities (not Bangkok, that is nearly two hours away). We are surrounded by family but many of them work away from home either on a daily basis, returning at nights or on contracts or business elsewhere in Thailand. In the immediate vicinity we have three married sisters and one married brother, all with grown families. They all have their own farmland and all work it in one manner or another according to their circumstances.

A week after I arrived, our closest neighbour (one of my brothers-in-law) got knocked off his motorbike on Christmas Eve on the main highway, coming home from work and less than 200m before turning into our side road . He spent the next three weeks in hospital with attendant disruption to everything. His wallet was stolen by one of the first people to the scene of the accident (yes, such things do happen in this, the most devout Buddhist country), and his wife spent many days and nights in the hospital to be with him, sleeping on waiting room benches or under his bed. Thai provincial public hospitals offer doctors and medical nursing but not much in the way of general patient care. They are not what Westerners are used to, at all!

When we arrived to live there were four dogs but we gave one away because he was being a bully, injuring other dogs and killing the household cats and he could not be controlled. Dogs and cats are not routinely given inoculations or maintenance medical care in rural Thailand. That's Buddha's job and they are considered disposable. One dog was nearly dead from liver parasites when we arrived, but after four weeks of daily medication she was on the road back again. Have you ever seen a dog with yellow skin? If she died we would have only had two dogs which is not an effective "security pack". So my wife bought three more dogs from her brother over the road in January 2014. There was one little bully in that lot too, so he had to go back leaving us with five, that's three of the original four and only two of the three new puppies.

Eventually the old girl who had the liver parasites sickened again and died, which was no great surprise to us considering how unwell she had been. This brought us back to four dogs, two adults and two pups.

We had bought a large cage with room enough for three small puppies to lie down and for bowls of food and water, but no thought had been given to the needs of three growing puppies. But, they had been living in a huge fenced yard and were not used to confinement. They could not just be left to run around free so they spent a lot of the first few days in the cage. However, they already understood house training and cried every few hours for a toilet and entertainment/exercise break, which came to be tiresome for both them and us, at the very least!

My boss (The Lady Of The House) had ideas of me building dog kennels, so we bought the wood and I started construction but realized with our personal effects shipment (including my necessary carpentry tools) due any day, I needed a more immediate practical solution. So the next day I went and bought some 20mm reinforcing bar and had it cut into 1.3 meter lengths. I hammered them into the ground, and with a 20 meter roll of 1 meter wide mesh made a 6m x 2m dog run using the aforementioned cage for internal accommodation, with a sheet or two of roofing iron to cover the cage for rain. The dog run was situated under some trees to provide protection from the sun. All this was achieved in one and a half hours after arriving home with the wire mesh and steel bars. I finished just before the truck came. Relative doggie peace and quiet for now.

Ah yes, the truck! It contained a large four cubic meter crate of our possessions from home, forty-four cartons full, and it had taken three and a half weeks to get here, a week to get out of the container and another week to get it customs cleared. Then they were not sure it was ours! What if they gave us the wrong crate, furthermore, a crate that had not even been customs cleared? All the packing case had on it (we were assured) was "Handle with Care" in English. How could they possibly be sure it was ours? This took an extra day.

When it was unloaded we saw that it had consignment note numbers written and stapled on all four sides, plus stickers with the port of origin freight forwarder's name. They wanted to charge us 500 baht extra for the truck waiting on the day they could not see the numbers, and would not deliver it till we agreed to the extra 500 baht. We had said "Yes" to not delay things further. So we unpacked as much as we had room to put away. About a quarter of it was clothes belonging to my wife but they mostly stayed in boxes for a few months because her wardrobe was full already. Plus a lot of kitchen stuff with no kitchen to put it in.

Ah yes, the kitchen! In August 2013 "The Lady Of The House" had come to Thailand for a month. She employed our first of four builders and drew detailed sketch plans for him to work from to convert the large existing OPEN kitchen/dining annex across the enclosed courtyard from the house proper, into TWO CLOSED rooms. As mentioned, one room was to be a dedicated kitchen and dining room and the other room was to become a day room for us, which they did first and it was excellent! The entire kitchen building was re-roofed as the roof was getting old and the leaks would have played havoc with our nice new plaster ceilings.

Some of the work was done by, or subcontracted out by a local guy that my wife calls "the glass man". He arranged the re-roof and the plaster ceilings. His normal business is making and installing custom glass windows, doors and partitions, so he did the sliding glass partition between the two new rooms and the floor to ceiling glass wall and door, opening from the day room onto the enclosed courtyard.

As soon as my wife left Thailand at the beginning of September, the other builder started doing a Frank Sinatra (I did it my way!) in the kitchen, and totally ignored the dimensions and location of the brick and tile benches in the plans she drew up for him. But, as she was getting progress pictures from his iPhone, it was not very long before the pictures told it all. He was told to leave the job and wait until we arrived in December. He agreed, and on arrival we had contacted him and he agreed to take up where he left off, as soon as he completed another job in late January. We were happy to wait that extra few weeks.

Since early August (for five months now) the family had been cooking in the garage as the exiting kitchen had been demolished. As the kitchen/dining room half of the old open kitchen/dining area was now an unfinished construction site, they used our finished day room as a dining room. This remained until we arrived and got the various construction projects back on track. Unbeknown to me, the part of the garage temporarily being used as a kitchen impressed my wife as a great location for a separate Thai food cooking area to keep all the stir-frying and boiling of dog and cat food out of the new area which could now become a "Falang kitchen". Hence, my use of the word "various" in describing the kitchen projects.

We put air con into the day room area as soon as we arrived in December. Wifey already owned a big wall unit with a hole big enough for a 40 inch Samsung HD Smart TV, so we bought one of those and moved the wall unit from the house into our new day room. Things were looking up. All we had to do was get our electronic toys and entertainment gear working and integrate all the stuff that had arrived from home in the aforementioned big crate.

Broadband was satisfactorily installed with a 12 meter high ground-station aerial attached to the two-story house roof. We had Wi-Fi all around the house and a cable from the modem to my old desktop computer that we installed in the day room. I will not bore you with the full details of making our TV actually work properly, or the circus that occurred when we installed the subscription-free cable TV which was going to have both Thai and English channels. But, after about three weeks, a techno-savvy nephew eventually managed to get the new Smart TV to work by changing the TV default start-up language to English and then I could switch on the Smart TV features. I unpacked my old desktop computer and fired it up in the day room as an entertainment hub using the TV as a 40 inch High Definition (920 x 1080) LCD monitor.

The much vaunted cable TV indeed gave us over 300 channels (if you count multiple duplicates) but only of Thai soap operas, Thai game shows and Thai shopping channels, none of which provided the Western mind with any great inspiration. The only "English" things were the occasional Western language movies in various Euro languages, but subtitled in Thai. The mouse and keyboard on my computer proved quicker to drive than using the Smart TV features on the big Samsung Smart TV remote, so I simply ignored the Smart TV functions and started using the internet connection for news as well as entertainment on my new 40 inch HD computer monitor! My eighty-two year old mother-in-law still had her own connection to the Thai cable TV over in the main house so at least someone important was happy. Samsung are now slowly dismantling the Smart TV features, one by one, anyway.

Incidentally, after two years I have still not got round to getting a proper English Language cable TV service with Discovery, BBC and National Geographic! I don't watch sport, and as now I can get movies and news by "other means" the need has receded, but perhaps soon... But never mind, with broadband installed we could now have Skype... Yeah Right! It actually took over a month to get Skype running because Skype had been bought by Microsoft and all new Skype connections started needing a Microsoft Account Number in order to log in. Shortly after getting my MS account set up they suddenly disallowed my password and would only repeatedly send me an online link to log a new password, which of course required my existing password access in order to change it, which of course was now disallowed! American technology at its best! Several emails and some weeks later, Microsoft agreed to a live phone consultation and a very helpful Spanish–American person fixed my password problem via a voice chat link.

Almost everyone in Thailand uses Gmail, Hotmail or Yahoo, and no one has ever heard of "internet server protocols" because they all use these "cloud" programs and the in-out protocols are all invisibly embedded in the browser interface. I wanted to continue to use MS Outlook as my mail account. This is "computer based" mail rather than "cloud-based" mail. After weeks of being told by experts in three countries that "this or that change" to my internet protocol settings would work, I gave up. Essentially I could have saved months of time and frustration if I had listened to my son-in-law who told me to use Gmail for everything and keep my home email account parked for $5 a month in case I ever decided to move home again. Months of hair-tearing later, I was forced reluctantly to follow his advice.

I tried to set up bit-torrent P to P (pirated movies for you non-tech folk) on my Windows Seven notebook computer, but my anti-virus had a hissy-fit over the bit-torrent software and I did not want to risk losing the use of my ACER portable, so I took all bit-torrent stuff off that machine. It all works fine on my old Windows XP desktop machine that was now a dedicated entertainment centre, so with the (small) virus risk of bit-torrent access, it makes sense to keep it away from my "work" computer.

Computers aside, the concept of being busy in Thailand does not automatically guarantee that you actually achieve much. Until you understand your Falang impotence in dealing with Thai bureaucracy and logic because you insist on using your culturally unsound Falang ideas, you often find yourself just running round in circles as if you have one foot nailed to the floor. For example, we are on our second bank now. The first bank guaranteed us a joint account with two separate EFTPOS cards... until the account was opened. Then it became, "Sorry, *Mai Dai*," (cannot do). More wasted time. Typical!

Anyway, enough enlightenment about all our problems with everything electronic and the complications with all the Falang stuff that came in the crate. It was now time to get back to trying to organize the renovation of the old homestead. This provided, as you will see, or had already guessed, huge opportunities for frustration, hair pulling and thoughts involving suicide and culturally unsound murder plans.

Chapter 4

Building starts again

By this stage our builder from six months ago was due to return but, as I explained previously, when my wife rang him to confirm his start date all he would confirm was that he was not coming. So, we were back to the drawing board again. We had names of other builders but they were all busy for several months and we really needed someone "RIGHT NOW". While we waited for our builder, and then started looking for another builder, I carried on with my plan to renovate, insulate and line the upstairs walls.

The upstairs of the existing farmhouse was of typical Thai farmhouse format. The exterior is painted vertical planks with battens overlapping the joints on a wooden frame painted inside and out, but not lined on the inside. The roof is asbestos cement sheets only three years old as it had done its thirty odd years and was replaced three years ago. There was no ceiling up there or fly screens on the upstairs windows except for "our bedroom", a section of upstairs that my wife had sectioned off and prettied up with really thin plywood walls and a nice paint and wallpaper job for our holiday purposes shortly after we married eight years ago.

Because this bedroom had never been insulated, we decided to re-designate this existing bedroom upstairs room into a guest bedroom and create a new insulated bedroom for ourselves, add an upstairs lounge and enlarge her Buddha prayer room. Our "new" bedroom would incorporate the walk-out balcony that already existed but was never used. Despite having the balcony rails strengthened and the balcony floor sloped and tiled, it still does not get used. Large fruit trees adjacent to the balcony tended to minimize the view while maximizing the access of flies, fruit flies, mosquitoes and other biting insects to our tender body parts. The dream of relaxing out there in the evenings with book and beer has unfortunately remained... just a dream!

Late note: In November 2015 that huge jackfruit tree was felled and I will be interested to see if it has eased the biting insect problem out there in the evenings.

Before moving over here I had decided that the upstairs area needed plasterboard wall lining, a plaster ceiling, window screens and insulation for the new wall linings and ceiling. I was aware that the timber framing upstairs had obviously been "cut on site" and then lined up to the outside cladding to provide a flush surface to attach that cladding to. Thus the inside surfaces of the "studs" (the vertical timber building supports) and "nogs" (the horizontal timbers connecting the vertical studs), were not lined up in any way. Major work would be needed before anywhere upstairs could be lined with plasterboard, which is NOT very forgiving.

Staff were not available by any means for at least the first five weeks, so I bought a Hitachi planer to carve off the oversized studs and nogs, and an 8ft by 4ft sheet each of 4mm, 6mm and 10mm plywood to make 1.5 inch (38mm) strips on my new Chinese table saw, to build up the numerous shallow places on the studs and nogs. There was neither a true vertical stud nor a straight wall anywhere in the entire upstairs part of the house.

Downstairs had concrete walls and wooden shutters but no glass windows. The second-story floor was composed of one inch thick planks of various widths and lengths that had been recycled timber when they were installed thirty odd years ago. They creaked and groaned as we walked around up there, and dust found its way between them and dropped down on the folk below. There were, however, nine main support posts upstairs, eight on the exterior walls and one central one so I worked between them and tried my best to make sections of flat wall, if necessary, independent of adjoining sections. Obviously I had to be very careful of nail heads when trying to plane off the hardwood studs and nogs with my nice new high speed planer to avoid destroying its cutters. This is where my chisels set and my Renovator tool (as seen on TV) would come in handy for excavating-round and beating-down, or removing, nail heads now the the household effects had arrived with all my tools.

I decided to just carry on by myself lining up the framing and insulating walls until the builder arrived in early February. I decided the best method was to insulate the walls with laminated polyester foam and foil sheet, as you will find that almost no one uses fibreglass "bats" over here and the thin laminated foam and foil sheet actually has a higher "R" insulation rating anyway and is much less attractive to pests. I planned for me (or builders when they got here) to staple one layer of aluminized building paper to the studs and nogs, to line each individual "box" on the inside of the cladding, and then staple cut-to-size sections of laminated insulation foam into each individual wall box. For this purpose I had shipped my two commercial grade staplers from home in our crate of effects, with 5,000 staples for the heavier one which was unfortunately too heavy duty and wanted to drive staples right through the exterior wall cladding. So I went to every hardware and major stationery and bookshop I could find in a 50km radius, trying to locate staples for the smaller Rapid tacking stapler. Absolutely no success and, as is typical in Thai retail, no one offered to look at my industry standard Rapid stapler and make a phone call to get the correct staples in for me. Eventually, in a moment of inspired desperation, I waved the staples and gun under the nose of the owner of a small school book stationer in the tiny village 4 km from our home and he had thousands in boxes under the counter. Go figure!

I had no illusions that a suspended plaster ceiling would be beyond me, but I realized until the builder arrived that I had a number of things I could do on my own. I could straighten and line the walls myself and possibly lay a plywood floor over the existing uneven, noisy, non-tongue-and-groove planks. I felt I may even be able to frame-up the new rooms by taking care in the demolition of the existing walls and reusing some sections of wall-framing semi-as-is. Reality struck home when I realized that I could not get even the plywood upstairs without cutting it in two or three pieces. No 1.2m x 2.4m sheet of ply or plasterboard was going to get up that staircase without being cut. This meant scores of awkward and heavy sheets of ply and plasterboard were going to have to be manhandled up 12 feet (3.7m) from the ground, over the balcony rail and then turned on edge to get through the balcony door. This would be totally beyond the only two able-bodied residents (me and my wife). Add to this the heat under that fibre-cement roof with no ceiling yet. It was coming into the hottest time of year and reality finally kicked in!

I could not do it alone!

Yes, I could have divided the job into two-hour days and taken up to a year to do it, but we could never have got the materials up there with me, my wife and one or more of her sisters doing a couple of sheets every day or two as needed. Builders were going to be arriving in a few weeks to do all the other work and I was only going to carry on by myself until they did arrive. So, while we looked and waited for builders, I decided to limit my duties to a few hours a day up there in the cooler parts of the day, demolishing flimsy plywood walls and laboriously trimming and packing the studs and nogs for eventual plasterboard walls. My decision was vindicated because our eventual builders used three, and, where available, four people to get those sheets up there. Two below and two leaning over the balcony rail from above, the two lower guys using a Thai scaffold section as a halfway house to pass the sheets up from. The rest of my time waiting for builders I spent with my wife planning how we were going to prioritize eight years of overdue garden maintenance.

Oh yes, there was still the orchard and garden to deal with! We had nearly two hectares (five acres) of orchard, mainly in mangoes and jackfruit, and lots and lots that needed to be done. The irrigation system had been done on the cheap, mostly many years ago. In other words it was mostly not buried, i.e. exposed to the sun. Sunlight weakens polythene and even standing on it can totally destroy it in seconds. All pretence of using correct fittings had been abandoned in favour of economy, using instead copious applications of black

3M plastic electrical tape instead of the correct fittings. This is by the way the standard way of repairing black polyethylene irrigation pipe, but even T or Y joints had been crafted in this ingenious "Heath Robinson" manner, and they were all leaking or broken.

There are three sizes of black polythene pipe in use on our farm, feeding water from a family communal dam over the road through a series of 2 inch blue PVC pipes and dozens of blue and red ¾ inch plastic ball valves. The ¾ inch ball valves feed ½ inch or ¾ inch black poly pipelines down the tree rows and 1/8 inch black poly feeder pipes carry the water to the actual watering nozzles. No single shop in my part of the country, not even the biggest places, has a full selection of all the irrigation fittings we use. By shopping around, I can eventually get everything I need. You have just got to ignore the Thai "NOT HAVE" answer, keep showing them "images" on the smartphone and then say thanks, then have a look around the shop yourself and if you cannot see it just go to try another shop.

Thailand is a bit of a literary desert if you are Falang and a reader, and I am both. Libraries if they exist, are not for Falangs, and out here in the rural countryside, well, you can guess. Bookazine and Asia book shops are great but are only to be found in major centres and it costs a lot of money to buy as much as I like to read. So I got a Kindle! I toyed with buying one at home before moving to Thailand but had decided against it. I should have bought it. They are dearer in Thailand and were almost impossible to find. The staff in the biggest electronic malls in the three biggest local regional centres were consulted and universally failed. At that stage, they had never heard of Amazon or Kindle readers. Kindle is a bit better known now, but as Kindle does not offer Thai language, and Thais are not big readers anyway (comics, yes, books not so much), it was almost totally unknown back then. They were reputedly available only in one or two special shops in the capital, but that involved a trip to Bangkok and probably a night in a hotel, so I decided to order one online.

I found that (I think courtesy of being a Gmail user) I already had an Amazon account so I researched Kindles and ordered a Kindle

Paper White from Amazon. They waited until the order was completely finished before telling me that they do not ship to Thailand anymore. So, I went onto "Kindle of Thailand" and behold, I had an Amazon account there too. Delivery was essentially next day to my door by EMS. Lots of free stuff and relatively cheap stuff came with it. I consider it to be a great investment, but in fact any tablet with the Kindle app on it would be great if you already have a tablet or iPad-type product. Kindles with their paper white screen use next to no battery juice and one charge lasts for weeks and weeks. Using a normal tablet as a reader needs a recharge every few hours and is not as easy on the eyes as the Kindle screen. My Kindle has stopped me going insane here and I love it.

My next set of notes for my newsletter for the folks back home, were created only a couple of weeks later in the last week of February 2014. By then we had a builder of choice telling us he *might* get to us in early March, but we decided we needed to get going if we could find someone else in case he took another job and never came. (Builders always prefer new work to renovations.) It was starting to get really hot and I was having to limit my time spent working upstairs anyway.

At about this time I made two saw horses as described in Part two, from plans I found on Google. I needed a working surface at Falang height because I could not work squatting as Asian workers do and you cannot buy saw horses in Thailand for love nor money.

We also found some local builders at this time and we started their labourers onto demolishing the wrongly built kitchen benches while the so-called carpenters took over from me upstairs. They kept all my work done so far and added a heap of stuff I could not have done as quickly without their compressed air nail gun and multiple staff working full days.

In two days they had finished off all my demolition and wall straightening and were about to start fixing plasterboard. Window awnings had been made by my wife's so-called glass man and were due to arrive sometime in the next week or so to cut down the window leaks upstairs in heavy rain. I installed self-adhesive foam sealing strips in the bigger vertical window gaps. Some brands stick and some don't but in Thailand there is no after sale guarantees, so trial and error is the only solution. Buy the Australian brand "Raven" over the Chinese brands. The gaps at the tops of the upstairs windows are big enough that they all let daylight in. The awnings are to cover these gaps and take rain away where it used to flow down the outside walls and be pushed in by the wind over the tops of the window frames. The glass man was also booked to install window insect screens upstairs and additionally make and install awnings over the most leak prone windows downstairs as well.

By this time I was starting to have concerns over one of my design features: laying plywood over the untidy, noisy, recycled timber, upstairs floors. Plywood is apparently made in Thailand but it appears to all be of appalling quality. The ply I bought in 4mm, 6mm and 10mm sheets to make wall shims up to pack out the studs and nogs to hang the plasterboard straight was terrible. It looked OK on the outside, but inside was full of voids and spaces. I would set my new table saw to run 1.5 inch (37mm) strips out of my sheets, only to find some of them disintegrated as they came off the table saw. Lack of entire sections of veneer layers and glue inside the plywood sheets was the problem. Sometimes I would start using a strip I had cut, but as I tried to cut it again to the desired length it would fall to pieces in my hands.

I was getting very nervous about what quality of plywood I would be able to buy for re-surfacing the floor upstairs. Fibre-cement sheets were suggested by the builders and others but would have looked terrible and the floor would not have been stiff enough to tile. I tried everywhere but all the plywood I have seen in Thailand, even now, looks to be of the same poor quality. I now know why the builders questioned my wisdom of even considering it. If there is good plywood for sale I have not found it, even a year and a half later. Trying to get good quality 12mm to 15mm plywood for my floor seemed impossible. Everything we looked at in timber yard after yard was obviously unsuitable. Most sheets had obvious (from the outside) internal flaws and many did not actually have even one good side, which is necessary if people are going to be seeing it or walking on it. The rough construction grade ply in the packing case that we shipped our personal effects to Thailand was two, three or perhaps five times the quality of the best we saw anywhere. One of our builders enthused about our packing case plywood and wanted to buy it for making furniture! I eventually used much of it to make shelves and internal cabinets under the benches in our famous Falang kitchen. So maybe he was right. Maybe it really was furniture grade packing case plywood, after all?

Eventually we drove to an obscure yard on the outskirts of a city about an hour's drive away and found some ply that appeared slightly better (or less really bad) than any we had seen elsewhere. AND he let us hand pick our forty odd sheets. And it was STILL really poor quality next to what we know overseas, but better than anything else we had seen at any price anywhere. But we were desperate by that stage and at least we had the right to hand select our sheets. We supervised it being loaded onto the truck and we drove home behind the truck. The quality was not great and after being installed our builders still sanded right through into voids in places on some sheets which they then had to fill and then stain.

All this sounds expensive but labour and most common building materials are remarkably cheap in Thailand. Labourers work for 300 baht a day, or even 200 baht a day in the north of the country. So-called "tradesmen" charge maybe 500 to 1,000 baht or so per day. That's a day, not an hour! The plasterboard wall lining, stopping and painting the whole upstairs (150 sq meters floor space) cost about 32,500 baht including materials, labour and paint. The suspended ceiling with insulation foil applied to every sheet individually cost only around 17,500 baht. About 4,500 baht bought each of our eight foot wide curved, colour-steel window awnings, installed. Nice looking door lock sets cost from 250–350 baht, heavy duty stainless steel door hinges, sets of three, only 175 baht. Sealant, silicone, or paintable acrylic is just 50 baht a tube. A 42 inch fake gold plate and five blade timber fan and light fitting for the new bedroom 1,875baht. Just out of curiosity, circular fluorescent fittings are still available in late 2015, complete with tube, ballast, starter and decorative glass cover from 159 baht (about $US4.00). See what I mean?

By late February 2014, my notes say, *Humidity is horrendous. I simply could not live here without proper Falang (foreigner) protection and comforts. Still no rain but it did fall 4km and 3km away at the end of last week, but NOT here! We get the lovely sea breezes after they travel over 30km of parched farmland and they are not lovely any more except in the evening and then you need mosquito screens to appreciate them.*

Other items at the end of February 2014 included new plans to upgrade the garage/packing shed to include a Thai kitchen, a storeroom and hobby workshop, and improved cladding. The garage walls were just huge lengths of whatever second-hand timber planking was available tacked up willy-nilly onto uncertain, sometimes termite infested posts. There were no doors except an internal one into the courtyard and any animal up to dog or goat size was free to walk in and out of the garage, packing shed and temporary kitchen, day or night. Upgrading the packing shed was a big job with concrete block walls and concrete topped benches right along the inside of the Western exterior wall, and with outside storage under those benches that would haunt us with our first termite infestation within six months and eventually, two more infestations within fifteen months.

Plans to add a toilet and shower upstairs and change to a proper septic tank were abandoned owing to the cost of this additional work and lack of confidence in something that complicated for these builders. My same notes say that dog training was well under way. Thais do not whistle but I had all five dogs (at that stage) responding to me whistling. The two puppies we got in January were coming to whistle or name.

Chapter 5

Water or lack of it and other matters

By late July 2014 all the jobs mentioned above were done and in addition we had the old concrete tank stand demolished as it was collapsing and rebuilt, with a roof added, and in a better position. We had the builders lay a concrete path around the last three sides of the house, 1.5 meters wide and totalling about seven cubic meters of concrete. This miserable episode is described in detail in a later chapter in Part 2 of this book, under "Building in Thailand". The two kitchens are both working well and the dining room is at last in the kitchen, leaving us our private day room. Yippee!

The refurbishing of the garage included lining the roof with asbestos cement sheet to make it quieter in rain and cooler in summer. Additional insulation was added in the ceiling over my workroom and the Thai kitchen. And a huge lockable steel sliding gate was suspended into place, cunningly and conveniently constructed so that one or two of the smaller dogs could still get in and out through the bars at will. That was NOT the plan!

We had put a lot of discussion into what sort of income we could get out of the property if we really put some planning and effort into improvements. Eventually we decided that the 200 mango trees on about 35% of the property needed to go as they had been fatally attacked by big stem borer while my wife was living overseas with me for nearly eight years. They were not the best market variety of mangos anyway so they went and several hundred hardwood trees were planted in their place. The plan was that they would reduce the amount of space we were trying to manage if there were just us (i.e. mainly my wife) and occasional help from family. The hardwoods with a very long growing cycle would add long-term value to the property, and the mangos had to go anyway as they were ultimately dying with the large stem borer infestation. Unfortunately, not long after we planted the hardwoods the government banned the sale of all new hardwood timber to stop legal sales being used as a cover for stolen or smuggled timber. This, plus the realization that we really could not do it all ourselves forced us to rethink management strategy as regards the whole property and this area in particular, and this unfolds in chapter six.

At about this time, The Lady Of The House was keen to get some lime trees planted on a section of the property near the farmhouse that had been back filled three or four years ago as a potential house site. It was a very big house site I might add, big enough in fact for several houses or one hundred lime trees in 80 cm concrete planters and twenty or thirty jackfruit trees. So against our plans for a year of rest and recreation after completing the house refurbishment, the boss wanted to get straight on with the orchard work to start it generating an income, so that is where our upstairs furniture budget went, for now. And that is what we mostly did with our time for the next six months. So during June, July and August, the diseased mango trees were felled and hardwoods were planted in their place. The first eighty lime trees were planted in the so-called "house site" area that we reallocated to them and another twenty were planted in gaps in the same area over the next year. Much of the detail of these activities is covered under specific headings in the later "farming advice" chapters in part two of this book.

In referring to notes dated 19th of August 2014, I got myself somewhat out of sequence as I lost two great friends in July 2014 back home, one in his 60s from cancer and one younger friend from complications twelve months after a massive heart attack. I knew about both of their conditions before I left, and while one was inevitable the other was a nasty shock. He was barely forty.

My own health after eight months in Thailand was the best I have been for years and I was consistently 6–8 kilos down on my pre-

Thailand weight. (At twenty-three months in late 2015 I am down 12–13 kilos on my pre-Thailand weight.) I put this down to country air, moderate outside exercise and both a change to, and reduction of, diet. First up, a huge reduction in intake of bread. Personally I think the importance of the reduction of bread in the diet cannot be understated. The family cooks with the best grades of rice and mixes at least two together and I eat some rice in two or three meals a day. The glycaemic index of the rice I now eat must be greatly lower than that of the bread I used to eat, and let it be understood that I never ate bread for two or three meals a day back home. I may eat a lot of rice but it seems to not be as fattening as bread, for me anyway.

In the heat humans tend to eat less, and in the cold we tend to eat more. For a variety of reasons at least one or two days a week we end up missing at least one meal, sometimes two. Going anywhere in rural Thailand involves long distances and a long time travelling. Sometimes we get up and go out early for some matter associated with the house or property, perhaps take coffees in the car with us and have a late breakfast somewhere which becomes brunch. On occasions we then get so busy we forget to eat again 'til we get home in the evening and then it is too late. So, we either have a snack, or, not wanting to go to bed on a full stomach, and perhaps not being hungry, we don't even eat dinner. In the hot climate I do NOT get hungry when I miss meals like I did back home.

Also, notably, I have had almost no flu or colds in Thailand. My first flu here I caught from my wife after thirteen months and everyone who got it took three to four weeks to shake it off. Because we were due to do major overseas travel we both jumped on it and had two or three courses of antibiotics to deal with the usual bacterial co-infections that accompany flu (which is a virus and impervious to antibiotics). We were still not over it when we flew out, but tickets were paid for and travel in other countries was part of the trip already, and involved other people and other arrangements so desperate measures were needed. Back home I would "catch something" and have to go to the doctor every three or four months, every year, before we made the move to Thailand.

One of my first jobs here was going to be to find a local GP but generally there are not many English speaking doctors and most Thais go to a hospital if they need medical help as they can then be referred on to different clinics within the hospital if it is urgent. And most Thais cannot afford to go to a doctor unless it is urgent. My home country had a lot of allergy things in the air that have caused me lifelong allergic respiratory problems which are notably absent here. Whatever I was allergic to back home (which extensive allergy tests never managed to identify) is simply not growing or in the air here. I had got to the point of having to do daily sinus rinses with saline over the last few years and even was supplied a sleep apnoea machine by my National Health Service back home, to help me breathe and sleep better. I stopped the daily sinus rinses and using the sleep apnoea machine a few months after arriving here. Incidentally, this is still true even in "polluted Bangkok". I now sleep better and snore less but losing weight helps that too, of course.

I have had to give up wearing my expensive hearing aids in Thailand because the heat makes my ears sweat inside and the discomfort drives me crazy. My ears became really difficult to keep clean and healthy, and the easiest solution is to just not wear hearing aids. Only rarely is anyone here talking to me other than my wife and I can usually hear her quite easily. Most of the time I ignore people talking around me because they are always talking Thai and I only pick up the odd word or two anyway.

I am lucky to have had normal blood sugar, normal blood pressure and almost normal cholesterol levels all my life. The one thing that really worries me about my health in Thailand (apart from a major traffic accident injury) is the possibility of suffering either a stroke or heart attack, and with an hour's drive to the nearest big hospital offering comprehensive emergency treatment I just might not survive it. I have resolved to have a full check-up and stress ECG annually and have returned to taking a small heart aspirin every day. The heat and humidity in Thailand are a pain for me but it is manageable. It can get unbearably hot in the middle of the day during much of the year and I am now in my late 60s and therefore not keen on overheating myself and causing a heart attack or stroke, which I think would be really easy to do in these temperatures.

The first two rainy seasons I have been here for were predicted to be low monsoon years. 2014 and 2015 have been pathetic. Nowhere near the usual monsoon rainfall has arrived for this time of either year but parts of the north and north-east suffer from the tail end of all the typhoons that have been pasting Taiwan, China, Vietnam and the Philippines and they have had some severe flooding upcountry.

The government has admitted that the water shortage in 2014 and 2015 has been exacerbated by serious flooding in 2013 which frightened upcountry dam managers to over-release water in the first quarter of 2014 out of fear of more damaging floods, for then the third flooding monsoon season in a row. Of course the result has been water shortage for these two years, because of poor monsoons. Severe water shortages look like being a problem well into 2016 and possibly beyond. If you are planning on settling in the north or north-east you had better get used to ongoing water problems. It will seem to you like you are always suffering from either drought or flooding in many parts of the north or north-east. Thailand has abundant water and usually plenty of rainfall but conservation, reticulation and storage need billions of baht spent on them and probably will never keep up with demand. Dig a well and build a dam or a storage pond (called a tank, here!).

As I write this segment of the book from notes dated the 8th of September 2014, news back then was that both the Mekong and Chao Phraya rivers were likely to burst their banks. That particular crisis passed and thirteen months later in October 2015, the Chao Phraya river was showing sand bars in its upper reaches in places not seen for decades. The Mekong largely borders Thailand to the north and the east, (running from north-west to south-east) passing Myanmar, Laos and part of Cambodia. The Chao Phraya is the important Thai river that runs more or less through the middle of the country, and bisects Bangkok before flowing into the gulf.

Unfortunately flooding does not usually equate with increased water storage. A storm from the South China sea can cross two countries and the resulting deluges can and do flood towns, villages and cities including parts of Bangkok most years, but it is usually in the wrong places to direct any useful amount of this excess water into dams or reservoirs. The storm passes, the rivers subside and the dams are still low. Recovering water storage in critical dams, rivers and aquifers can take up to two or three years. Some aquifers only contain ancient water and have a recovery time calculated in thousands of years or more.

Chapter 6

Heat, farm carts, dogs and lawnmowers

I have a nice suntan in Thailand as it is nowhere near any "holes in the ozone layer" and it is therefore safe for me to rarely wear a shirt around home unless we have visitors, or I am going to be outside for more than five minutes. Then I wear a white T-shirt and a big hat, but I come in when I get too uncomfortable. By that stage I am usually saturated with sweat so I have a shower and do something else for the hot middle part of the day. I am doing quite well with the heat really, but there is no point in pushing it. My wife is younger than me and of course, somewhat better acclimatised than I am. If it is too hot I stay mainly inside where we have air con in our bedroom and the day room. I can read or work on one or other of the computers. I have downloaded lots of movies, documentaries and umpteen seasons of *The Big Bang Theory*, *Mythbusters*, *Cheers*, *MASH and Hill Street Blues* etc. I can see no point in being a hero or an idiot in the heat.

With all the rain up north we decided not to do our Laos trip yet (mid 2014). I went to Laos twice fifteen years ago in January each time, but my wife has never been there. We keep promising ourselves to go to Laos and in a moment of stupidity were thinking of going in the middle of the year. Then I realized two very good reasons for NOT going as and when we were planning. (1) Laos is very steep and has very bad and dangerous roads. Steep, dangerous roads and monsoon rains. Hmmmm! (2) Monsoon rainfall and dengue fever and malaria mosquitoes. Those are two very good reasons to leave it until at least October/November, or even till later in the dry season, perhaps in 2015 or 2016 sometime.

I restored a Thai farm cart off our farm scrapheap during August 2014. These take the form of a low flatbed platform about 80cm square with a robust water pipe handle at the rear and with side frames on the cargo deck. These sides keep any load from engaging the two heavy duty, wire spoked, bicycle type wheels which are positioned just slightly rear of centre. They have a smaller wheel at the front and, with no load on, the point of balance makes these carts slightly nose-heavy. They are great for moving baskets or cases of fruit, bags of fertilizer etc or any large bulky load that will fit and are not overweight for the construction of the particular cart. It had belonged to my mother-in-law and had never been designed for loads more than say 50kg. It had been left outside for several years and was in very bad shape.

I found some phosphoric acid based rust killer at HomePro and cleaned it up and then had a bit of welding done on it to replace some rusted out members and had the front wheel replaced. New tubes for the tyres, new wheel bearings and a careful de-rust and repaint of the spoked wheels and frame. I did the whole job, rust kill, sanding and painting at a total cost including all parts, welding and materials of about 900 baht. Shortly after completion some builders working on the property borrowed it to move a lot of heavy stuff and overloaded it, bending the frame. They had a welder so I hammered everything straight again and gave them some sections of 1 inch OD box section steel tube I had lying around and told them to fix it. A bit more painting and it may be a bit heavier, but it is now stronger than ever.

I restarted on my dog kennel/s several times (or tried to) over several months but my wife kept changing the specification so much that I stopped. And a year later I have not started again. The dog population at current time of writing is now seven. The old female with liver damage died and about that time we raised and domesticated two semi-wild pups we were given by a friend who needed to get rid of a whole litter from a property she was selling, and on the 1st of December 2014 we got "Lucky" at one day old. This is covered in Chapter 7.

So we have seven dogs and there are no kennel plans that we have looked at that, will work for containing seven dogs, short of fencing the whole property, fencing off a whole dog yard (which is useless for property security) or building a dog village with individual kennels and chains that are far enough apart that they do not entangle each other. Currently our dogs roam free day and night and the only thing I can think of is that it will remain that way till we fence the whole area we want secured over the next year or two.

The next major acquisition was a lawnmower to control the grass and weeds on the property. We have a petrol powered two-stroke weed whacker (line trimmer) but it is relatively slow, tiring to use and much of the land is reasonably flat and clear. We purchased a 21 inch Honda self-propelled "walk behind" mower at the end of August 2014. It was highly recommended by a couple of people on thaivisa.com as being the best and most reliable machine. They are highly regarded by mowing contractors in several countries. The cost was around 24,000 baht but after running the motor for nine months it now does nearly four hours on a tank of petrol. The only thing I have had to spend on it so far has been the replaceable cutting blades. Like many things not made or assembled in Thailand, parts are a ridiculous price here and the blades sets are between three and four times the price here than in many Western countries.

If you decide to buy an imported machine of any type, or for any reason, and it uses replaceable blades or similar parts, consider arranging a source of supply and delivery for these items. We use it a lot so we eat around three to four sets of blades a year at the moment but hopefully they will last longer when we get permanent staff in and start to keep the ground clear of sticks and stones that hammer my blades. Most of the year we mow the property, usually over three or four part days, every two to four weeks. However, during the wet season that grass grows faster than we can mow at a ½ inch (1.25cm) a day at least. We then have to get ruthless and get a contractor to spray the grass with weedkiller. This knocks the grass down for a couple of months and it comes away again at the end of the monsoon and we resume mowing.

Chapter 7

We need staff and a staff house. Building again!

But the property was taking up too much of our time. There was land not being used for productive income and we have done none of the travelling we planned, and there is too much dirty, heavy, repetitive work for us (mainly my wife) to do, long-term. The answer was always that we would have to employ staff. But, Thailand has a labour shortage problem. Official government figures estimate it is short by several hundred thousand workers and these numbers are topped up by guest workers from Myanmar, Laos and Cambodia. By September or October 2014, we came to the conclusion that the property would take all our time and still not give us a good income and we really needed reliable local staff for the long-term, but more immediately, as we needed people to water and maintain the property while we went for a planned overseas trip together for five weeks at the end of January 2015. But, because we live in the main industrial growth region of Thailand, we are always in competition with factories for workers so farm labour (which pays lower than factory work) is always losing staff to factories and no reliable local staff seemed available. We tried on occasion to get local people to help my wife with knocking the property into shape but only drunks and layabouts applied. And even in desperation, when we gave them the job, they failed to show up to start work. No one local wanted to work for us and the workload was really telling on my wife. This shortage of local staff had formed part of our original plan to operate on a smaller scale and not employ staff. But the small scale farm model was an impossible dream, the work piled up and it became obvious that we (she?) simply could not do it. The problem of dry season watering in January–February was really "the last straw that broke the camel's back". How could we attract staff and compete with the region's factories?

One cunning plan to attract staff we had was to provide a reasonable staff house to try and entice a married couple who like the outdoor life. We were hoping to find someone who perhaps for family reasons will trade a few thousand baht a month for an outside job that comes with decent accommodation including free water and power, particularly if there are children involved, as a good school is within easy walking distance. My brother-in-law was using a builder at his house over the road, building a rental "resort' type house on his property. The builder was about to finish there and had no other contract to move onto and wanted more local work as he lived locally. They were happy with his work (slow but careful) and so we tried him out, extending the roof of our new brand new (four month old) water tank stand to join up with the house and provide more covered outside space near the second "Thai" kitchen. He certainly was slow, but, working on a contract basis, we were happy with the result. In the meantime we drove around the local area and identified properties with staff houses. There were quite a lot of obvious worker houses in the area and they were almost universally just atrocious dumps, thrown together out of reject scrap timber with grass roofs or fourth hand rusted iron roofs and/or sides. Frequently they were located on the side of rice paddies or fish ponds to provide staff accommodation and security as well. It was not hard at all to tell the difference between most owner houses and most staff houses. The worker houses looked like abandoned emergency animal shelters.

So, we took a deep breath and started our new builder onto a "semi-deluxe workers house" about 20m west of the main homestead. It was to be a 48 sqm concrete block cottage with a 1 meter raised concrete path around it and a good fibre-cement roof. We planned two bedrooms with a small combined lounge/ kitchen/dining area with a separate bathroom. It would have been very nice. My wife fancied that she could get it all done for 150,000 baht but I knew it would be closer to 250,000 baht including extras such as access. Unfortunately it needed access, so twenty-three truckloads of fill later, plus two days with a small backhoe at 5,000 baht a day and we had a drive, a culvert installed, some stumps removed from the building site plus the toilet waste tanks dug and installed ready for the house to be built. The house kicked off in late November 2014 with nine concrete poles, covering 8 meters by 6 meters. It was to be largely completed by late January 2015 when we had our first trip planned to return to our other home for business and other reasons.

On the day we were making the access road for the new house, my brother-in-law's gardener (from over the road) appeared in our new drive with a newborn puppy in a small bowl about the size of a soup cup. This was our introduction to Lucky. He had been born just the day before. His mother had lain on, and smothered to death, the other six pups in the litter and then she died from loss of blood. He was the only one out of the eight to survive. That is why we called him Lucky! My brother-in-law was away on business and the gardener said if we didn't adopt the pup and feed him he would die. We fed him with goats' milk from a plastic syringe every few hours for weeks, and the staff and family kept going with the milk and finally weaned him off it while we were away in February.

We kept Lucky in a cat-sized plastic carry cage for most of the first six weeks with a muslin cover over to keep the mosquitoes off him and, of course, at the start he was blind, helpless and unable to walk. But from almost the very first day he was self-house-trained. If he wanted to toilet he would cry when he heard us in the garage and fall out the door to pee-pee as soon as we opened the cat carry cage door. In fact the only time he would wet in the cage was between his last feed at night and his first feed the next morning. Within a few days, well before his eyes were open, he would growl and bark at any strange voice in the garage. Our six other dogs including two females all liked him as a newborn pup, but no one wanted to be Mum, Auntie or Uncle to him. We had three six-month-old male kittens in the house and we told them they had to be uncles to him. They big heartedly took it in turns to tolerate his rough-house puppy-games and his attempts to find milk nipples on them. Lucky, not surprisingly, has turned out to be an excellent guard dog but became incredibly bossy and stroppy with the other dogs even as a small puppy, a problem which continues. He has no respect for his older kennel mates and sadly, all three of his kitten "uncles" have vanished, one at a time, over the ensuing year.

If raising our new orphan puppy was going well, then raising the new house for potential staff which started on the same day was not going so well. In fact it started to go wrong very quickly. Our builder worked well, if slowly, by himself but proved totally incapable of managing the staff he hired to build our house, and he neither could he bring himself to organize his need for building materials. The first we knew was always "I am out of…" and work stopped until it could be supplied. He had some financial disaster in a job a few months before ours and had lost a lot of money and equipment, so he had very few of the things he needed for the job. He had to borrow some very basic tools from me! They started well enough but within three or four weeks productivity had started to slip. We could see there was no way the job was going to be complete on time. We had nine poles up, the perimeter foundations poured and steel work starting for the roof frame in roughly twice the time it should have taken him and his team.

Neither our builder nor us knew on any given day if he would have staff or not, and, if so, how many. The pattern started that we would pay them every few days and then lose them until the money was gone and they returned with a hangover. One was eventually hospitalized with alcohol poisoning and discharged from hospital to live in a temple. Completion date slipped to perhaps late March or early April because we could see that work could not possibly proceed while we were away. Who would order and pay for materials? Who would pay them for appropriate work? And then it suddenly got really complicated!

We had put the word out with friends who had contacts and had found staff for themselves and others before. Through them we were put in contact with a couple who lived about 100km south from us who seemed interested and we discussed salary offers over the phone and a March/April start date. We were in the process of getting them to come and look at the property and discussing other job details. Suddenly, about a week before Christmas 2014, we got a phone call from them that the wife had lost her job as a rubber sap collector owing to the collapse of the rubber price, and with the job they also lost at about one week's notice the house they lived in on the rubber farm. They wanted to arrive on Christmas day 2014, with two children and take up the job immediately, accepting our conditions and pay offer, which as a first offer was deliberately a bit low. We never found an independent source of information about the cause of this state of affairs but advice from within our family all pointed out that if they were good staff, well recommended, we should not let them get away.

Chapter 8

One house becomes two

It was with some considerable misgivings that we discussed with our builder how we could speed up the completion date of the house and the options became clear. The planned house could not be finished before March/April but if we suspended construction on it he felt sure they could build and complete a smaller, simpler staff house somewhere else nearby in about three weeks, i.e. before we left the country. The option would then be to either demolish the work so far on the other house or complete it with upgrades to make it suitable for another purpose, possibly a rental home. This option would give us staff to do some general garden maintenance, but much more importantly water the orchard while we were away. About 60% of the property was already set up for semi-automated watering but not all trees needed the same watering frequency and the 2 inch (50mm) pipe could not provide enough pressure to water everything at the same time anyway. So, some manual turning on and off of the taps in sections was required every second day. The system had not yet been extended to water the hundreds of new hardwoods at the other end of the property and they would almost certainly die in five weeks of dry season weather that we would be away. We had already started supplementary watering there with two 50 meter hoses as November/December started moving us into the dry season.

We were certainly trapped between a rock and a hard place. We were faced with two scenarios: As local friends and family were not going to be able to fill the gap completely as regards proper watering, then we either had to get these staff on site somehow to water for us or expect to come back in late February to possibly hundreds of dead trees. A great selection of options... Not! We decided we could modify the garage with makeshift curtains and it would still be better than 90% of the local staff accommodation we had seen. Yes, our new staff could come!

On 22nd of December 2014, one year and five days after arriving to live here, we broke ground again digging foundations for a simple structure with nine shorter poles and most of the floor made of seventeen, four meter by 40cm precast, reinforced concrete slabs. This was my idea to speed construction. For his part the builder misadvised us into doing half the walls in concrete block and half in steel frame and fibre-cement weatherboards. Doing it all in concrete block would have been much quicker, much cheaper and much simpler regarding weatherproofing.

Termites: Episode One. On the 23rd of December, while starting the smaller staff house, the builder needed some concrete boxing timber that we had been storing in the outside storage area beside the rebuilt garage. This outside storage area is under the work and storage benches inside the shed, but the storage area "under the benches" is actually outside the garage (if you can understand that). He pulled out some timber and it was infested with termites. We immediately pulled it all out and we sprayed everything in sight with Chaindrite termite and ant killer. We then discovered that termites had crawled along a stress relief saw-cut in the concrete path laid four or five months earlier, and under a stack of wooden window shutters (from the rebuild of the old family kitchen) that were leaning against the side of the garage. They then found their way up a concrete wall, through a pinhole in the concrete workbench above the outside storage space, and into my new workroom. There they had infested the plywood topping that had been screwed down onto my concrete workbench to give me a nicer work surface to my workbench. I cut the plywood workbench top away in sections but they had got to the whole bench top and it all went out to burn. We thought we had found them just in time. I hoped that they had got no further and that all the infestation was contained in the bench top. I now have a plain concrete workbench top with twenty screw holes in it that used to secure my plywood workbench top. Little did we know that I was wrong and they had got into other timber. In less than six months we would locate a second, and even later, a third termite infestation in my workroom that would require much more drastic action. I HATE TERMITES!

The new farm staff arrived with their two children on the 26th of December 2014 and moved into our garage. Even for all this and the builders vanishing to get drunk for several days over New Year, the staff were able to move in to sleep the first night in their new home on the 17th of January. That first night, there were no windows and no power but by the time we flew out five days later, on the 22nd of January 2015, the doors and windows were in, the power and water were on and we had finished painting inside and out.

The builder had a bit more work to do to tidy up the new staff house and we agreed on what work he could do on the bigger house while we were away. We paid him in advance and he decided to lay off his troublesome staff and work on his own while we were away. He wanted to bring his brother who was a more experienced builder than him (that should have been a hint) and his brother's staff when we got back. Our builder had work and money to tide him through and we had staff to water our trees. We travelled with clear consciences and rang back to Thailand regularly.

But back to our new staff. Right from the start, somehow things didn't quite ring true. The wife was a good worker and understood tree care but the husband seemed to have had no experience and exhibited little enthusiasm for either work or learning anything about the property or the job. Within days they had started trying to re-negotiate their employment and indeed tried to impose their own conditions. We agreed to raise the pay rate which was against the agreement but was, as a first offer, too low anyway. But, all we could think was "Things are going downhill already. This is not going to last." It was clear that we were being used and they had no intention of staying in their new job and new home. We knew that the government was currently deciding whether it was going to subsidize rubber prices, and if it did agree we realized she would find a rubber tapping job and they would be gone immediately.

While we were away the government did decide to subsidize rubber selling at 39 baht a kilo by 21 baht a kilo to reach the magic figure of 60 baht a kilo, and our staff immediately demanded from our family a holiday right then, despite the fact that we told them they had to wait for us to return before they went away from the farm. Over the phone from overseas we said, "No Holiday," but immediately a relative or friend "reportedly died" and they went to the funeral regardless. To no one's surprise, on their return it transpired that they had been "offered a job while at the funeral". However, it had rained big time for two days while they were away, so much rain in fact that our family advised us that the property would not need watering again until we got back in ten days' time. When our staff returned they tendered notice and asked when they could leave. The reply was, "Right now if you like, and pick up your wages after the owners return." This is when they were due to be paid anyway.

Chapter 9

Back from overseas and a new builder

We returned from our trip overseas on the 25th of February 2015 to live trees and no staff. To his credit our builder had completed the roof steel work on the bigger house. He had also installed the roof sheeting and done his best to brace the nine concrete building posts against possible wind damage which was possible with the roof in place acting as a big wing sail. He had also done a modest amount of other work but according to family had not been around much in recent days. We arrived very late at night on the 25th of February and did not venture out much the next day. We had become somewhat disappointed by the quality of his staff, his control over them, his inability to plan for ordering of materials and finally some of the advice he gave us during the construction of the smaller house. Then he vanished for two or three days and during that time we noticed a number of items that we considered poor workmanship and remembered the problems we noticed he had, getting the foundations of both houses square.

We began to discuss between ourselves that he might be working beyond his capabilities in doing a whole house. A handyman carpenter he might be. A house builder he might NOT be. He re-appeared again after two or three days so we sat down for a meeting and confirmed our intention to continue with the house but assured him we needed to work more closely with him to assure we got what we needed. He in turn sat quietly and offered no contribution to the discussion and no news about his brother and family as replacement staff. Then he went home and again did not appear for another two or three days. Enough was enough! We packed his gear up, took back all the tools he had borrowed and handed everything else to him when he showed again. I think we had a lucky escape. We consider the job was too big for him and he did not realize his limitations till he had made mistakes. Whew!

We did not know what to do next. Then after about a week one of our preferred builders from the original farmhouse refurbishment contacted my wife. He had not been available seventeen months ago in August 2013 when the kitchen rebuild had started. And we had not spoken to him since. But he was available now if we wanted him. Thank you, Buddha! He started immediately, about the end of the first week in March 2015.

We launched into a revised build of the original staff house, moving the kitchen and bathroom area into a three meter extension to the rear of the house. The toilet waste tanks had to be moved to clear the three meter deep extension and the bathroom was split into two bathrooms with a separate wash and vanity area. The house was changed from two to three bedrooms with the master bedroom bigger, and an entryway added on to the front. More fill was needed and compacted as extensions to the front of the house moved the building forward down our gently sloping property. The entrance to the house was getting higher at the front and an elegant porch with surround seating and a car park area was added. This extended the house to 120sq meters indoors, plus paths, car park area and a beautiful front porch making a total "footprint" of around 200 sq meters. The original budget was out the door and 100 kilometers away running for its life.

As the property is gently sloping and has a large catchment area behind, it can be subject to flash floods during tropical storms at any time of year but particularly in the monsoon season. My wife told me that on occasion water has flowed over the property in extreme downpours up to nearly half a meter deep in places and I wanted to build to deal with this if, or when it happened. I was concerned about walls and foundations being undermined in such conditions. If you have seen water move downhill during monsoon downpours in Asia you would understand why I had raised, backfilled concrete paths built out from the walls, 1.2 meters on all four sides and included second foundations at the edge of each path. The house foundations, the paths and path foundations all were tied together with steel reinforcing to prevent the outflow of water from the properties behind, reaching our house foundations and undermining the house. The builder had never done anything quite like that before but understood and executed my instructions perfectly. In the tropical storms that came during September and October 2015, the house handled the water exactly as we had planned.

One of my original ideas to help keep the house cool was to use a 3 meter ceiling height instead of the more common 2.4 meters. Several people had commented on how much bigger it makes the house look. They also commented on how cool the house was, even during construction. With light exterior colours it may not need air conditioning at all or just perhaps in the master bedroom. This guy, our fourth builder, has been a pleasure to work with and we have no recriminations about any of his construction work. As soon as the paint was dry, the "glass man" installed his windows and the electrician completed attaching all the fittings. The builder's last work, after painting, was the connection of water and wastes on the 7th of September 2015 and the house was handed over to us. He would be building sheds on an adjacent property for family and would tidy up any paint details, sticking wooden windows and doors. In the process of connecting the water to the new house we decided to install a 1,000 litre water tank, and using a spare pump we had available we were able to provide some dedicated water storage to the house and improved water pressure. These last-minute items were completed over the last few days in the same week.

Termites: Episode Two. Four months before the new house was completed, I started having this funny feeling that termites might be somewhere in the old main house building or storage shed/garage as a result of last year's rebuild and improvements. There was no reason for my premonition. I just had a hunch and the feelings kept getting stronger. In what I thought was an unrelated matter, the door to my workroom started sticking; getting hard to open or close! I was starting to get quite suspicious about the west and south walls of my tool room, its ceiling and the garage ceiling, all of which were hollow, framed with timber and closed in with fibre-cement sheeting. I was even considering making small inspection openings to view into them. One evening as I was on the verge of knocking inspection holes I mentioned termites to my wife and she hit the roof. "Don't worry about it! You worry too much about everything! We do not have termites, etc, etc!"

If you are guessing that the next day, the 29th of May 2015, I found termites, you would be right! They were in the doorframe and walls of my tool room. The door frame to my tool room was collapsing, causing the opening and closing problems and I caught them just starting to burrow from the doorframe into the door itself. And, if they were in the doorframe, the hollow walls were obviously infested. When we rebuilt the garage we had all the old timber roof joists and posts in the garage painted with Chaindrite-1, a creosote-based anti-termite treatment and most new construction was now concrete, steel and glazed tile. The exceptions were the east and south walls of my storeroom and the doorframe that the previous builder "made". All of the original garage timber was genuine Thai hardwood and therefore moderately termite resistant and we had reason to be very glad we had insisted that all existing timber was painted with the anti-termite treatment.

I had to carry and stack all my tools upstairs and remove all my shelves and racks. Then the walls and doorframe were demolished. When I started removing cladding, both the hollow wooden framed walls were riddled with termites in just twelve months, with their muddy trails going up, down and sideways. As we pulled everything down, termites poured out of every hollowed out piece of timber like so many grains of wriggly rice.

Our current (Number 4) builder pronounced that a previous builder (Number two) had used some termite infested timber to make the door frame and for the bottom plates of two walls. I agree with that opinion because of the muddy termite tracks radiating out from certain pieces of timber indicating that they were the source of the infestations. The termites had gone up to the roof joists but fortunately had not attempted to penetrate them because of the termite resistant treatment we had insisted on and the Thai hardwood timber there.

Over the next two days, the 30th and 31st of May 2015, the builder rebuilt the walls with concrete block after I sprayed everything with termite spray. After the concrete dried I gave it a few days to cure then sealed and painted it. The build took three men two days and cost just 5,000 baht in labour using blocks and concrete from the house site, plus paint and a new doorframe.

Because of the extended building program there was no opportunity for us to leave the property so we had "managed without" staff over spring and summer, with the intention to recommence looking for staff on the completion of the house construction in early September. We have found some part-time local help and utilized gangs of up to fourteen migrant workers in "blitzes" on certain projects for one to three days at a time, when we found ourselves hopelessly behind schedule. With the final upgrading of the irrigation system to be complete by the end of September, almost every tree on the property will be able to be watered by turning section isolating taps off or on and switching on the pump for hourly sessions, then swapping other taps on and off for subsequent sections. Live-in staff were still our "long-term goal" as I finished this book but we did find a local man who comes in daily and fulfils our requirements for now.

Termites: Episode Three. On Sunday the 23rd of August 2015 I discovered termites for the third time in my workroom. This time they were in the window frame and they were my fault. In December 2014 we found they had crawled up through a pinhole in a concrete bench top and infested my plywood workbench top. The bench top touched my workroom window frame and I had to remove and burn the bench top. As we were trying to build a whole new workers' house in the next two to three weeks and staff were arriving to live here in three days, I didn't go looking for problems and had to hope for the best. They had infested the window frame from where it had touched the bench top and away we went again. Did I mention that I HATE TERMITES?

On finding them this, the third time, I ripped out more wall lining and sprayed the window frame more thoroughly. The builder was on a mission to finish painting the house so I checked that the damage was localized and waited until after the 7th of September when the house was officially finished. The builder then came over, checked the walls and ripped down a small strip of ceiling over the window. No more termites were apparent. There were still a few alive in the top rail of the window frame but we killed them and put the window frame on the fire. Everything in that area, except the wooden shutter windows, is now made of steel, concrete and fibre-cement sheeting. There is nothing for them to eat except the wooden shutter windows and no muddy tracks were leading off anywhere else. However, as we were finishing installing the wooden shutter windows, I saw what looked like termite "muddy" just visible under the edge of a window hold-open stay fitting, and yes, they were in one of the two wooden shutter windows. We rushed out and bought another one of those and the infested shutter went on the fire too. That wall lining and ceiling can stay open for a while until I feel good and confident to close it in again.

Thirty-six years ago Neil Young and Crazy Horse released the album "Rust Never Sleeps". I would add "Termites" to that. They are astounding for their stealth and destructive capacity.

Chapter 10

More water works

The time-line of writing and editing this part of the book is October and November 2015 and nearly every farmer in Thailand is very concerned about the availability of water over the next two years. The disastrous actions of running down the water levels in all the major dams in the first quarter of 2014, plus at least two very disappointing monsoons (in 2014 and 2015 so far) has created a drought through much of Thailand.

Our main irrigation water source is a large deep artificial pond, a "tank" as we call them, which we share with one other family member but every year the tank silts up a bit more and both the pond owner and us are adding more trees that need water. One day we expect there will not be enough water for both our properties without a major re-excavation of the pond sometime in the next few years. We have a low volume shallow well for household use and a bit of irrigation and there is a disused well presumably on the same water table only twenty-five meters away. The household well cannot run for even an hour without a rest to refill it. The volume is fine for our current uses but water production is too slow to be used for irrigation without storing the water up first. We tried to get a well drilled a month or so ago on a no-water no-pay contract but the rig was old and unreliable, and after a whole week they only got to sixty meters and then had to abandon the well as layers of fist sized white quartz rubble nearly trapped their drill tooling down the well. We had high hopes of our own independent high volume deep well to give us a chance of independent water over the next year or two and for the next sequence of drought years. The failure of this well was a great disappointment and we still lacked any form of independent water source or storage.

Our builder was completely finished with building the house for us, and waiting for a temporary power connection to a property close by where he is to build a large storage shed and perhaps another small house. We had discussed with him building a pair of 2 meter wide by 3 meter high concrete tanks to hold the water from the well. These would hold just over 19,000 litres which is a handy buffer for a few days in an emergency and we were planning to connect to our new well to fill them. Despite the failure of the well, we decided that independent water storage is better than no emergency water plan at all, and as a last resort we could probably truck water in to the tanks in a crisis to save our orchard from fatal drought while we tried to get another deep well drilled.

So we decided to get him to build the two tanks to give him a job while waiting for electricity on the next site, and they were finished on the 2nd of October 2015. We had no immediate complete strategy for the tanks but obviously we needed to connect them into our 2 inch farm water reticulation system to use any water in them at all. On completion of the tanks we went to fill them and found that the previously disused well next to them had improved with our recent use and pumping and although it is on the same water table at 10 meters, it refills much faster than its twin only 25 meters away upstream that we use for household water. It is much more suitable for our purposes than we had dared hope, but it may just be a meter or two deeper than its twin 25 meters away and therefore just hold more water than the household well. In the dry season, under full production, it may thereby "steal" the water from the household well which would not be desirable. We think it is unlikely that it will pump as well during the dry months as it did at the end of the monsoon!

The water from the well is cleaner than our pond water and will wash out our pipes and supplement the pond supply. The 19,000 litre concrete storage tanks provide part of the solution to our long term water independence and it remains to be seen if we need to attempt another deep well or not. During the construction of the tanks we were referred to another well driller with a more modern rig who knows about the other well failure but is confident enough to almost guarantee a successful well. However, the ground was too wet to drill then so we elected to defer that option, but it will be an available option if the recently re-commissioned shallow well does not keep up its volume during the dry season. We will have to wait and see.

Water from these tanks is above our land and fed by 3–4 meters of gravity. The first 2 inch pump we bought to replace the stolen pump (see below) was not powerful enough and we had to buy another one. This first pump was now sitting in our shed but it is nearly too powerful for this application at 600 litres a minute. At present with gravity assist from the tanks it can empty both of them, all 19,500 litres in well under an hour. The first few days of December found us tweaking the final details of the 2 inch connections and float switches to patch the well to tanks and the tanks to our irrigation system.

During the same two month period since the completion of the house, two other noteworthy events have occurred. One of my wife's sisters finally gave up trying to juggle her domestic duties helping us, our joint eighty-four year old mother, minding a granddaughter and her husband's full-time job with the responsibilities of maintaining a two acre (five rai) mango plantation almost next to our land. She decided to give us a ten year lease on it at a very good rate and we have already pruned it, moved tons of new and old prunings away from the trees. This allows clear access to the trees which now have been sprayed and fertilized (with paid family help) for the first time in several years and we even harvested a useful out-of-season mango crop from it. New leaves are shooting away as I write at the end of November. It will prove very helpful to us for income support over the next few years.

We had some business with the local "Or Bor Tor" or elected councilman and my wife finally asked him about staffing in passing conversation. He has a brother-in-law who has spent a life in heavy construction work. His health in late middle-age will not let him continue in that heavy demanding work anymore, and he is pleased to have a less demanding local outdoor job in a more relaxed environment. He has health limitations which place some restrictions on one area of work but it looks like he is almost ideal for our requirements at the moment and he started work in mid-November.

We still have no live-on-site-staff but my wife's long-term plans for the farm include more intensive agriculture for which we will need reliable daily staff. Interestingly, since starting this local guy we have had several people offered to us as live-in labour. It is like as soon as you buy a new major appliance, when several people say: "What a pity. I could have got it for you wholesale."

However, our vacant staff house and our new independent water storage (now all connected into the farm water distribution system) give us two of the most important components for future developing increased production on the property, as we get to them.

Essentially this finishes the first part of this book and in part two we move onto specific advice for people wishing to become "A Gentleman (or Gentlewoman, for that matter) Farmer In Thailand".

Part Two

Chapter 1

So you would like to be a gentleman farmer in Thailand?

Before we get too far advanced, let us discuss your role in any farming endeavour in Thailand. And, for the record, let me also explain my part, and my limited qualifications to be giving this advice.

The purpose of this book is not to give you a university degree in Thai farming. It would have to be a much bigger book and would need to be written by someone way more qualified than me. It is intended to point out the good and bad things about the lifestyle I have chosen and, if the circumstances should arise, to help you make such decisions for yourself.

Every year thousands of foreigners come from overseas and "experience a holiday romance" in one of the main three or four main tourism centres of Thailand. Many of these people fall in love, or at least temporarily in lust with their new Thai friend who frequently does NOT call the tourist centre they met in, their real home. If the relationship becomes serious then the choices boil down to "your country or mine". Many people from cold climates like the idea of living or retiring if possible in a "tropical paradise," and for many people, Thailand fits that bill. However, many would not choose to live their whole life in a tourist centre and the Thai person (woman?) frequently has the dream of "going home to live". Home is where the family is and it is overwhelmingly common that they come from a rural village or a family farm in the country, usually in the North or North East of the country. A Thai Buddhist upbringing focuses heavily on the responsibilities of the sons and particularly the daughters in a family to provide and/or care for the parents, particularly as they age.

So, if the new romance is to blossom in Thailand, not the tourist's home country, the tourist (you?) will have lots of questions. If this is you, and you are wondering what it entails and whether you could handle it, then this part of the book was written for you.

I am a retired sporting goods retailer. I have family involved in dairy farming back home, my father was a civil engineer and I have always been a bit of a DIY (do it yourself) kind of guy. I am a curious person and I love to read a lot. I make no claim to be an expert in farming in any country so I will try to restrict myself to general background advice to the fellow amateur farmer. There are many things that we Westerners take for granted in our own country but become downright confusing in an alien country with a foreign language, written and spoken. The advice I give on transferring money, land area terms, crops, irrigation, wells, electricity, water storage, suitable clothes, shopping for farming/hardware supplies etc are all things that are as I found them. If your experiences are different to mine then that is probably due to local cultural habits or local variations of some type. I hope you enjoyed reading of our adventures and challenges in part one of this book and can profit from our lessons and advice in part two. You may even decide that a farming life in Thailand is not for you. In that case then it was better for you to find out sooner rather than later!

There are many books and websites including the official Thai Government Immigration website that explain more about the legality of the situation you will find yourself in, but in short you certainly will be exactly a gentleman farmer because you are not legally allowed to work, even on your own farm in Thailand. Besides, it cannot even be your farm. Because it must belong to your Thai spouse or to a company or other person or entity in which you may only own a maximum of 49% of against 51% to someone else. As a foreigner you are not allowed to own land or work on it. You may own a condo in a large block that does not involve your own specific piece of land.

But by working on "your" farm you would be taking a job off a Thai person so it is nominally impossible to ever get a work permit to work on a farm, **AND an offence for you to be caught doing so.** And there are lots of Thai people who could do your job.

Of course your Thai spouse/partner can work on it, as my wife does but she is Thai. You will be allowed to provide working capital and presumably hold "directors meetings" to plan the future of the farm. You can count the money and possibly help take it to the bank. But, to comply with the strict letter of the law, you don't want to be found working in any role, including selling the produce at a market, repairing the tractor, ploughing, weeding or planting crops, pruning, spraying, watering or digging postholes.

Now, having told you all the negative, scary stuff straight up you may still decide to join our select club, probably several thousand strong, of men who love being "Gentleman Farmers in Thailand". I shall continue, by telling you more of the interesting, facts-of-life stuff and advise you that it is not all bad.

First up, the good stuff: You are presumably a Farang, the generic Thai term for any westerner or "person of white race" and as such:

1. You are not likely to be acclimatised to working a full day in the heat and humidity that exists most of the year in the tropics.

2. You probably have a lower tolerance to biting insects (various ant species), scorpions, mosquitoes (yoong), sand flies (lien), wasps and poisonous centipedes etc, than the average Thai manual worker.

3.   Snakes are everywhere in Thailand and some of us come from snake-free or snake-rare countries or regions and perhaps you are just are not used to tripping over them – <u>sometimes literally</u>!

4.   Many of us are over fifty years old now and consider that the quality of life that a gentleman farmer expects does not include "doing it all yourself" anyway!

5.   Labour is cheap in Thailand. Most farm labourers work for between 200 and 300 baht a day in Thailand. (I do not endorse near-starvation pay rates but simply tell it like it is.)

But you must approach this intelligently. Don't be one of the people who get over here, find they cannot afford to stay (or fall out of love with your partner or whatever), find you have spent all your money and have nothing to show for it. Also you may have nowhere "back home" to go back to, and no job prospects or potential income either in Thailand or back home. This scenario is very common and is not restricted to the "Gentleman Farmer" class. It has become an absolute disaster for many people with their money in a condo in Pattaya or Phuket, no income and a redundant relationship. If you are going to come and stay here with a spouse on a farm, remember that the land will be in someone else's name, even if you paid for it. I repeat, you can own a condo but you cannot own a farm, land, a house or even shop-house if it is on its own land. You will hear about companies with 51%/49% ownership but remember you are the 49% and have very few legal rights here. Even if the 51% is with a Thai lawyer, just remember the stories about all the crooked lawyers back home. I suspect there are also a few crooked ones here. It would be like waking up during a house fire and finding someone has stolen all your clothes

Make sure you know the person well before getting involved at this level. This is obvious but circumstances and relationships change. You will be most secure if she already genuinely owns the land and your investment is only some improvements and/or you have been together a number of years so that you know and trust each other completely. This takes time. Not nine months of sex-deprived emails following a two week whirlwind romance in Pattaya.

My wife and I were married and living together for almost eight years in my country before we came over here and we had joint business and household bank accounts for years back home. My wife is not a drinker, does not gamble and had no complications of adult kids by previous marriages. Not even a secret, greedy, ex-husband. What I am saying here is be careful! Alcohol, drugs, gambling, a greedy family, or an ex, or the spouse's dependents can all be fatal in Thailand. They can make you very poor or even totally destitute in a matter of a very few months. I'm not joking. Follow *Thai Visa Forums* for a few months and read the horror stories. Think with the big head, not the little head, as they say.

So, how does a Pattaya "hotel receptionist" get to own farmland. As Thai farming parents age, as in Western farming cultures, land is frequently divided among the children of the house. This of course can involve female children as well as males becoming land owners, but like in Western cultures the kids also want their own "Big O.E." (Overseas Experience). Whether this is construction work in Dubai or hotel reception work (or worse) in Bangkok, Pattaya or Phuket, it means the son or daughter may not be living near their land for one or several years.

This is why you will quite often find Thai folk (male or female) working in the tourist areas who in conversation will claim they "have land, back up home". Beyond the hoped-for excitement that draws young people off the farm and into the Big O.E. or big cities, there are frequently other factors at play. The land may be big enough for a house and small garden but not large enough to operate as an economic unit. Or, the lack of good paying jobs locally means that the owner cannot earn enough to build a house, or even find a decent paying job to provide a livelihood to live on the land if a house of some type already is on the land.

And there is the attraction of meeting possible partners away from all the guys and gals they grew up with who now have accrued the common rural curses of dead-end seasonal jobs, drugs, alcohol and domestic problems. The ultimate dream for many is meeting and marrying a rich foreigner. This is like hitting the super jackpot, much, much better than winning a mere one million baht in the Thai lottery.

So, perhaps she owns land but works in Pattaya (or Phuket). If it is just rice paddy that is usually not very complicated. Someone just pays a few thousand baht a year to rent the paddy. Bare land can also be rented out to other operators to plant cassava or sugar cane, among other quick growing cash crops. A long-term tenant may fertilize the land because he wants good crops for the next five years. But, on a one-year lease he will do the bare minimum. If he plants several crops over two or three years the land may get handed back in a depleted state. Several (or many) truckloads of straw and manure may have to be spread and ploughed into the ground, as an example, to revive its growing potential.

If there are established long-term fruit crops on the land it gets more complicated. My wife's land had several hundred established fruit trees, mainly jackfruit and mangos. In most cases another farming member of the family will "look after" the land if the owner is out of town and not able to take an active interest in the property for one or several years. In our case her farm had been looked after by an older sister and had certainly not been allowed to die, but production had tapered down because the trees had not been kept pruned, watered and fertilized for optimal results. We probably did not provide much encouragement because at that stage we were planning and building a different future in a different country. Whenever my wife went back home she was full on into buying and shipping product to her other home and she had little time or energy to spend playing orchardist. In truth, at that stage we had no plans of ever coming back to work the property again properly. It was too much to expect that our family would maintain everything to optimum standards if we were not showing much interest. It is fair to say that the best person to care for anything is usually the person who owns it. Family members who are earning a living off their own land have to put their own priorities first, especially when the property area they are expected to manage has suddenly doubled in size. The good news is that although productivity may taper down, it usually returns a season or two after good farm management regimes are re-imposed by the returning owner. There is a heap of catch-up work to do but the property can be brought back up again.

Back to relationships. Every person when meeting someone new that they are attracted to likes to make a good impression. We all know this. So if someone who is a new or casual acquaintance, talks of "my land" bear in mind that it just may be **"my communal family land"** that she or he is talking about. In a casual conversation this is just "talk" and no more. However, not everyone has the same threshold for detail or honesty and if a relationship starts to get serious then more and better information is required. You would not understand a Thai property deed even if it was shown to you and it may not even be up to date. But, to a large extent, time and trust will deal with many of these situations. However, in every family people are born, get married, break up and eventually die. Remember that family land can and does get moved around in these changes, but sometimes the paperwork does not keep up. People often choose not to spend money tidying up property documentation because it can raise unpleasant and confrontational discussions within the family. Lawyers and government paperwork absorb valuable time and money and if there are no obvious immediate benefits such matters can easily be deferred for years. Such situations probably exist in many families throughout the land so it is important to inquire into how land titles have been settled in recent divorces & re-marriages etc if there is a possibility that they may have some effect on the property that your intended owns.

Thailand has some complicated laws regarding owning and inheriting land between husbands, wives and children. I am no legal expert but I have been told the "percentage of a person's interest in a piece of land" can change with deaths, births and separations in the family. Many marriages are "village marriages" without a government marriage certificate, just to confirm and celebrate a relationship in the eyes of the families. If the relationship endures for a reasonable period, and no legal marriage exists, how is the "divorce" then to be handled if one of them owns property? It is a bit like "the verbal agreement which is not worth the paper it is printed on". Very often there is no malice involved and everyone knows the score, but a piece of land may belong to some other parties, jointly with, or separately from, those who occupy or farm it now, or whose name is on the title at the land office. If you decide to invest in your new love interest's land you had better try to be absolutely sure it really belongs to her (or him). You do not want to drill a well and build a house and barn only to find you did it for someone other than whom you thought you were doing it for.

The information you think you remember from an early discussion may not have been completely accurate. She may be under pressure by other family interests or have divided loyalties on the subject. Perhaps she just didn't realize or had forgotten what she already told you. Maybe you misunderstood. In our family there was one innocent misunderstanding caused by language difficulties. I believed for several years that a house belonging to my wife's brother actually belonged to her mother and father. Mum and Dad lived there and we always "went to see Mum and Dad at their home". It WAS their home at that elderly stage in their lives. Mum and Dad actually owned another house in the trees over the road but age and frailty made them move in with a son. Another son with his wife and daughter were living in the parents' real family home at that stage, but we had never visited Mum and Dad there. Now my wife owns that house and that land and there was no fallout from this situation. But, misunderstandings can and do happen easily where culture and language are alien. And, sometimes it could involve accusations of, or even actual intended deceit.

If you decide to go into farming or otherwise join lives with the love of your life remember this. You are a foreigner and you would have very few legal rights here in disputes over money, particularly if that money has been invested knowingly and willingly by you in a Thai citizen's land. I said this before, but it bears saying twice. You could go all legal with it but that is about as romantic as a pre-nuptial agreement and much less certain here. Good luck with that one!

Be careful with your money. Start slowly and keep your eyes open. Discuss together all plans regarding the property. Neither of you should run off and make big decisions or commitments without discussion and joint agreement. Develop a business plan for the property (it is a business now, one that you are investing in) and you need to draw up a capital expenditure budget. Prioritize expenditure and don't go building a flash new homestead if you really need a new well, a fertilizer shed and a new cultivator or tractor. In two months to four years, depending on what you have planted and if your relationship and the crop have both been satisfactorily nurtured, you should see a return on an investment that makes you both happy and hopeful for the future.

But, be realistic in your expectations. The economy in Thailand is more modest than in the West. Planning to reduce our dependence on money, say, from superannuation payments from home is likely a more achievable goal for most of us than making a fortune to live on out of the land.

Bringing your money over from home. Take it slowly. On *thaivisa.com* we frequently see questions about "the best and cheapest way to bring all my money over together". Why on earth would anyone want to do that? Bring only what you need for immediate circumstances and research the cheapest ways of importing funds from back home, but only as you need it. Just think about it and unless you come from somewhere really bad, your money is surely safer in your old bank at home. The bank interest deposit rate here is pitiful anyway so you can probably keep your nest egg invested better and certainly safer back home.

Chapter 2

Land and crops. Farming in the "Land of Smiles"

<u>Thais do not talk in acres or hectares.</u> They talk in "RAI". A rai is approximately .4 of an acre. That means there are approximately 2.5 rai to an acre. This is a convenient figure because by co-incidence it is the same ratio (approximately) as acres to hectares; 2.5 rai to an acre and 2.5 acres to a hectare. Or about 6.25 rai to a hectare if you prefer.

These figures are a guide for you, not exact. If the land is not big enough to be economic then there is not much that can be done without buying or leasing more land. I am not sure what constitutes an economic unit for rice but it has to be at least 20 rai and even then they will have to be growing a premium grade of rice to even begin to make money. The poorer grades of rice that some people have been encouraged to grow in recent years under the great infamous "Rice Scheme/scam" can actually cost more to grow than you can sell it for.

<u>Rice is Thailand's biggest crop</u> but it has become only a marginally profitable crop to grow and many people lose money particularly in drought times. In 2015 some rivers and dams ran dry in June and July before the monsoon arrived late instead of early May, and then arrived relatively weak. Many parts of Thailand can only make a profit from rice on two rice crops a year. And some parts of Thailand, particularly parts of the North East, are more drought prone than others and the water supply is not reliably able to guarantee enough to grow two crops. In 2015 and 2016 the government was and still is actually instructing people in some areas to NOT grow a second crop. Cruelly, in time of monsoon or heavy cyclonic rain, some of these drought prone parts can also become flood prone! And the water runs everywhere but into the dams where it should go!

Most smaller holdings require crops other than rice to be profitable. Crops that are cheap and simple to grow and are not as water hungry as rice, include sugar cane and cassava (also known as manioc or arrowroot). These crops are frequently grown by large commercial-level farmers who rent large tracts of land from multiple owners who cannot afford to farm, or for other reasons are not farming it themselves. They may pay as little as 1,000 baht or even less per rai, per year. If you are considering farming these crops they may not make much any than rice but there is relatively less work, water and costs in growing them.

On the subject of crops, some sample first harvest dates from crops are listed below.
(1)   Salad greens, chillies, melons and herbs: 6–16 weeks
(2)   Bananas: 7–10 months
(3)   Limes: 10–15 months
(4)   Quick maturing fruits e.g. passion fruit: 12 months
(5)   Most other tree fruit crops (Jackfruit, Mangos, Durian, etc): 4–7 years

These are not to be taken as recommended crops to grow. They may not even grow in your area. Just remember to keep some land to grow something short term to give you some income while the longer maturing crops come up to speed. Four or five years is a long time to sit twiddling your thumbs with zero income.

Note that not all crops will grow in all areas. And certain areas are "known" for certain crops or fruit. Our area is known for jackfruit, mangos, durian, longons and lots of rice. You need the correct crops or precise sub varieties that do well in your particular micro climate. Understand that there are many varieties of each basic fruit. Not all varieties of a given fruit are created equal. You must research which varieties have the best shape, taste and colour, will sell best, and are "fashionable" right now. And you must only plant varieties that for reasons of altitude, temperature, water demand, soil type, disease and pest resistance etc are suited to your area's microclimate.

Only buy from local nurseries you can trust. You do not want to wait four years to find you have planted the wrong variety of jackfruit or mango. Some unscrupulous folk will sell your partner the wrong stuff if she is accompanied by a Falang and particularly if they come from "out of local area". Remember, your vehicle number plate says whether you are local, or drove there from a long way away!

When the trees are coming to fruiting age there are all sorts of local tricks for maximizing the harvest. Water supply, fertilizer (animal manure and concentrate), pruning and spraying for pests all contribute to optimum crops. Hormonal enhancing sprays and other tricks can be used to bring on increased leaf and bud growth and even manipulate the time and duration of the harvest.

If you are taking over a new property, or "taking back one from a caretaker" that has been "unloved" for a while, you will have a range of work that will require attention, either immediately or ASAP. This will probably include pruning, spraying, repairing/replacing irrigation lines and feeding with fertilizer.

Lime trees come in a number of varieties and I do not advise you to plant them until you know exactly what types of limes are most popular in the area you want to sell them. The distinguishing features are (a) with seeds or seedless, (b) bigger or smaller and (c) cheaper or dearer. Bigger, seedless (Tahiti limes) which actually originated in this part of the world, not Tahiti, are more expensive limes and will not sell in low income areas, but may be fine for the more prosperous Bangkok or export market. Kaffir limes are grown for the double-lobed leaf famously used in Thai cooking, not for the fruit (which can be used but is not very juicy). Limes are best planted in 30cm high concrete rings, 80cm or one meter wide, several meters apart. The planting medium is 33%/33%/33% potting mix, dried cow manure and burned (black) rice husks. Irrigation is essential as is spraying as flying beetles and ants love them too. At different times of the year you will get between one baht and seven baht per lime. YouTube has videos explaining how to "force" the trees to fruit at the time when prices are highest, but we have not had time to go down that route yet. Lime trees start fruiting in less than a year, and at sixteen months should be cropping heavily.

Jackfruit can be good money during the December-April season, but require consistent maintenance all year round and create a huge amount of waste in culled fruit and dead branches. Thai jackfruit trees generally grow shallow rooted so they can fall over easily and need constant propping up. They can quite easily be badly damaged by storms. They suffer from much top branch die-off which creates pruning all year round. They also will produce many more fruit than the branches can physically support and the tree cannot possibly ripen them all to full term. There are two criteria for culling jackfruit. Only ripen fruit close to the ground for ease of handling and to also reduce the hazard of a falling 10kg fruit killing you. Also about half of the baby jackfruit are born with skinny stems which cannot support the weight of that fruit to full ripening. Cull the skinny-stemmed ones!

For culling you have two options. (1) Culling over 50% of the fruit all year round creates hordes of fruit flies if it just rots on the ground or; (2) allow the "cull" jackfruit to grow to a bit less than one kg (two pounds) each, and then cut them in batches. This avoids the heaviest drain on the plants ripening energy and you can get reasonable money selling one kg sized fruit to a canning plant where they are prepared as a vegetable. It is impractical to dig holes big enough to dump cubic meters of culled jackfruit and branch prunings. You will probably need a dedicated area you can drag pruned jackfruit branches to for burning. Once you get a fire going with a good ember bed jackfruit branches will burn well, even green and freshly pruned.

Mangos are also one of Thailand's premium crops but again, consistent work all year produces the best cropping results. My wife had 200 mango trees in the unirrigated section at the far end of the property. Unfortunately, while my wife was living overseas her mangos all got infested with a sort of giant branch borer and also termites underground. They were also not the current "best seller" so we felled several rai of nearly 200 mango trees in May and June 2014. Mango wood is desirable for smoking and making charcoal, so it was a slightly cash positive exercise as the wood, even full of borer, is worth slightly more than the felling costs.

Co-planting, replanting and cash-cropping. We originally re-planted that mango area with hardwoods to reduce the area we were managing when the hope was that we could manage the property without staff. But now we have had to accept that we cannot do it all ourselves, and staff have become an essential part of all our long-term plans. Therefore we want to use that area for some higher value fruit crops or updated varieties that will crop and sell better. Additionally, shortly after we had planted the hardwoods, the interim "coup" government introduced a law banning the sale of new hardwood timber to try and stop illegal logging. This left us unexpectedly in a situation where neither we nor future owners might be allowed to sell the hardwood anyway.

For this reason we will probably start to gradually remove these trees and "bag-up" the roots and keep them watered and stored so we can sell them for transport and replanting. Mature and semi-mature trees sell for good prices so it does not have to be a loss maker and could well "turn lemons into lemonade" for us. We should actually do quite well out of it, in fact. Individuals, corporates and property developments will be needing trees near us and not that many bigger trees are available in our province.

We really need to change to crops that we can see will pay wages to staff and provide a return for us. We have therefore re-planted in the older orchard to replace dead or damaged trees, trees producing old fashioned fruit varieties and trees that just are poor croppers. As the newer trees come on, we will cull damaged or non-productive trees over the next 1 to 3 years to get space and light for productive trees.

It is a bit of a juggling match to improve the property with more desirable or higher producing varieties and yet keep production flowing in the interim. You must plan to plant various crops that mature at different times so you always have cash flowing. Even chillies can be planted between rows or on edges to produce an off season cashflow crop at 100 baht a kilo. You may have to prune your trees a bit harder to let more sunlight in for the secondary crop. Papaya (pawpaws) and bananas also grow quickly and produce big, valuable crops.

Chapter 3

Developing the land.
Spending your money!

Water, Wells and Dams. Thailand is blessed with abundant water but conservation, storage and reticulation developments always run well behind demand. Also water mostly comes in drought or flood events and some regions (particularly the North and North East) have more problem events than others. Your own reliable water supply by river consent, dam or well is the secret to your independence from water shortages but it should supply all year and never run dry.

Dams or "tanks" as private deep artificial ponds or lakes are called, need to be excavated and deepened occasionally as they silt up with topsoil washing in with monsoon rains. Try to retain this soil on your property in a stockpile somewhere, somehow. It is your topsoil. Wells are quite reliable in some parts of the country but problematical in other parts unless they are very deep. Essentially there are two types of wells, shallow or deep.

Shallow wells are usually dug using a large backhoe and get down 10 meters or so. They are supported internally by around thirty stacked large concrete rings about 30cm in height and one meter or so in diameter and then backfilled around. In areas where these wells "work" many Ampurs, (local councils) have policy to dig them free, usually one per property. They work on an annual budget so you may book it now but not get it in "this year's budget".

Deep wells are drilled and are anything that a backhoe cannot reach to dig. They are narrower than shallow wells, commonly 150mm to 300mm in diameter and drilled with a well drilling rig and usually supported with blue PVC pipe walls. A good well typically can be 60–200 meters deep and supply up to 3,000 litres per hour. High production volume is needed from deep wells as the small diameter well cannot not "refill and store" much water as in wider "shallow" wells. Without high volume production you would need to pump water up from a well as it flows slowly in and store it somehow in order to use it. Commonly the well drilling contractors will drill a well and supply pump etc for around 80,000 to 120,000 baht on a "no-water-no-payment" basis. I have related our recent experiences with wells in part one so will not repeat it here.

Relatively inexpensive water storage tanks can be created on a reinforced concrete base by stacking the same concrete well rings used in shallow wells and plastering them together inside and out. Tens of thousands of litres storage takes up very little space and is the cheapest above ground storage going. Two stacks of ten, (total 20) two meter rings on a concrete base should cost about 45,000 baht for 19,500 litres of water storage. This price is storage tanks only and does not include any pumps or pipes required to make it all work.

Irrigation Pipe: The Black and the Blue: Water is reticulated around private land in BLUE PVC pressure pipes. It lasts for years, is non-toxic and can be protected from long-term UV (sunlight) attack by burying, painting or covering somehow. It is supplied mostly in four meter straight lengths (in six meter lengths for the ½ inch and ¾ inch pipe). It is jointed and elbowed by cutting and virtually instantly joining with solvent cement. We move all the water around our farm in 2 inch pipes and step down to ½ inch or ¾ inch flexible black polyethylene pipe for irrigating rows of trees etc. Mostly we use the ¾ inch size black "poly pipe". We only use the ½ inch, ¾ inch and 1 inch blue PVC pipe for moving water to and around the houses.

Black Poly Pipe (called alkathene in many Western countries) is quite sensitive to sunlight damage after a few years which means that burying it is desirable until you forget where it is and either you can't find it when you want to add a sprinkler, or you do find it accidentally by cutting it with a spade or digging hoe. It is a thin wall black polyethylene pipe, flexible enough for most gradual curves without collapsing. It is joined, elbowed and connected by heating the end with a little throwaway gas pocket lighter and pushing the warmed plastic over special very cheap rigid black plastic fittings, and by very inventive use of lots of black electrical insulation tape.

Black flexible poly pipe is cheap and reliable but suffers from sunlight. Many types of sprinklers are available but when connected to the thin 1/8th inch inside diameter feeder lines, we have given up on the ones with water powered rotating nozzles. They are fussy to clean and have several parts, which are rarely interchangeable even though they look identical. We have too much dirt in our water from the dam which is fed from road and farm storm run-off and we find the very cheap, fixed, one-piece blue, orange and yellow nozzles are more reliable for us. The different colour codes represent the volume of water they will spray in an hour. They still block but can be easily cleared with a home-made wire nozzle pricker, or easily and cheaply replaced, even with the water running. In our area we have lots of termites and I suggest you only use the proprietary black plastic sticks to support the irrigation nozzles. Bamboo sticks only last a few months in our area before they are eaten.

Bury both kinds of pipes wherever possible or paint them (particularly blue PVC) with a white oil-based house paint scratching with fine sandpaper and/or wiping the pipe with mineral turpentine first. Ultimately, it all eventually needs replacing but try to get the best life possible out of it first wherever you can.

Draining water away: Once again, blue PVC pipe is used because Draincoil, that wonderful, handy, perforated flexible drainage pipe used in all those French Drain videos on YouTube, is NOT available in Thailand. Much of Thailand is clay surfaced so water does not easily penetrate the soil. It lies in pools until it evaporates or runs away over the land and scours away all your banks and topsoil if you are not careful! Trap your water somehow in little shallow soil or concrete drains and carry it away in 3 inch or preferably 4 inch blue PVC pipes. Preferably 4 inch for tropical rain because anything smaller than 3 inch blocks too easily with just one leaf and a twist of dry grass. There is a cheaper lightweight grade of blue PVC pipe and fittings available that does not handle pressure as well, but it is ideal for drainage projects.

Natural fertilizer or animal manure. Chicken poo, duck poo and cow poo seem best. Pig manure is very good but I personally believe it is likely to include pathogens that are more easily transmitted to humans and I am a little wary of handling it. My wife believes that chicken manure is quite strong and should be used sparingly or diluted with soil or potting mix. Use whatever you can obtain in your area and which works for family and local friends. Just don't put it on too strong. A little and often is the way to go, preferably just before gentle rain is expected.

Animal manure needs to be mixed 1/3 or less with a cheap potting mix or topsoil and burned rice husks to put in the hole when planting trees or they can be too strong and kill rather than benefit your new trees. Potting mix is 15–16 baht a small bag at most plant nurseries; (900–1,000 baht for 60 small bags). Rice mills usually have mountains of burned rice husks available cheap and may even help you to bag it (to count how many you take). Regardless of the crops grown, most properties will straight away benefit from feeding to improve humus and increase fertility. If the property is planted in fruit trees and then you will need to organize a regime of fertilizing, spraying and pruning throughout the year.

Spraying with chemicals is necessary unless you are going to go organic which is praiseworthy, but you will need expert advice that I cannot help with. Get it wrong and bugs will devastate your crop and maybe kill your trees. Different crops need different chemicals for fungal and pest protection as well as different hormonal treatments for different crops and times of the year. Two-stroke petrol motorized knapsack sprayers holding 25 litres are available from about 1,000 baht and up. Local spraying contractors are usually available in every area or a neighbour who needs the money and has the time (and you can trust) could help you out. If doing it within your own immediate household members or your own staff be sure to outfit the person with appropriate safety measures: gloves, mask, boots, apron, back-spill cape etc and follow the safety directions pictograms on the packaging.

Chapter 4

Living and staying alive

Clothes to wear: I like to wear shorts and just a T-shirt mostly, but on very hot days I do not spend much time in the full sun in the middle of the day. At tre hot time of year, I wear one of those multi-coloured polyester knit balaclavas with eye and breathing holes on my head. Over this, hanging down over my shoulders and neck, I place a 50–60cm square of cloth cut from an old T-shirt or knit sports shirt, and I pull any wide brimmed hat onto my head to hold the square in place. It provides extra protection for the neck/shoulders area and stops sweat running into my eyes. At certain times sandflies are a problem and they like to bite me round the eyes and I am allergic to them. Spraying insect repellent over the balaclava eye and nose holes a few minutes before putting it on keeps them away. In the early morning and evening, when it a good time to walk around and look at the property, mosquitoes are a problem in some areas, particularly if you are in a dengue or malaria area. Then you must wear long trousers and exercise serious precautions!

Socks: Ordinary nylon dress socks and slip on rubber sandals keep many biting things off your feet. Biting ants get their feet tangled in them and can only crawl on them relatively slowly.

Gloves: The cheap woven fabric white or green-grey gloves are sold in bundles everywhere and look like they are not much use, but they provide protection from many ant bites as the ants' feet get tangled in them, the same as with socks. They also keep your hands clean especially when pruning many fruit trees that have sticky white sap. They can be washed and re-used. Leather gloves are necessary for machinery, chains, ropes etc, AND for protection against snakes, scorpions and centipedes when handling logs, rocks, rubble and stacks of building materials.

Insect repellent: "Deet" is the world standard best chemical name to look for on personal insect repellent packaging. Some others, including organic plant extracts, work for some people.

Internet and phones: Thailand has a modern cellular telephone network with a number of competing service providers. Smartphones are the way to go now although some people still use simple cell phones with limited abilities. Once you realize the handy features hidden in a smartphone you will never go back. The camera and internet data features are very handy when buying stuff for the farm (see the chapter on shopping). Good phones are not expensive and are getting cheaper every year. If you do not need the expensive features, you don't need to buy the top brand/model phones. Dozens of brands and hundreds of models of "Android" system phones are available at budget prices and the system is intuitive and really easy to use. Apple and Microsoft phones also excellent but are generally dearer. Apple and Android are probably easier to use than Windows phones but Windows 10 may be changing that. I just love the Android system pioneered free from Google! Install one of the free security systems to protect you if your phone is hacked, infected or lost/stolen. AVG and CM are free market leaders but there are and will be many more others. Install a super hard glass cover for the screen (300 baht or so) and get a good robust cushioning case for it so it survives if you drop it on a concrete shop floor.

Many country roads do not have telephone wires anymore. Ours were cut down and stolen years ago for the recycle value of the copper. You might have to learn to live without a wired home phone. It is the way of the future so get used to it. The other way of the future to get used to is broadband internet and Wi-Fi. If you are a dinosaur and don't understand these terms you need to learn fast.

With broadband you can have free weather reports updated even half-hourly to your 3,000 baht phone and you can make free or almost free calls to almost any phone in the world on the same mobile phone, take pictures and HD video and send them too by a variety of available programs using something called V.O.I.P. to anyone, anywhere, all for about 600 baht a month for your Wi-Fi broadband connection. I use Viber and use Line occasionally. My wife is the opposite. She just lives on "Line" and uses "Viber" occasionally. Oh, the SIM card in your phone also lets you use it as a phone when you are out of reach of your Wi-Fi.

The only catch is that sometimes in the country there will be places where trees may obscure you from one internet provider's aerial tower, but usually there is another provider who you can access, or in extreme cases you will spend 5,000 to 20,000 baht for a really tall tower of your own, but it is a one-off cost and then you are connected like everyone else. It happened to us when a growing spurt hit some rubber trees near our home at the end of the 2015 monsoon and we were without internet for about six weeks. It was hell!

Let me say this. I would have great difficulty living without broadband now. It has become an essential service and as telephones computers and TVs grow together, more interesting and indispensable things will be possible in the near future of broadband.

Electricity in Thailand is extremely dangerous. If there is one thing I want you to remember from this book, it is that in Thailand electricity is very dangerous. It is usually installed by unqualified people who buy protective charms from the temple and treat electricity with contempt, with predictable, tragic results. Many existing homes including ours had no earth and were wired using two core cable. If two core is used they might run a separate thin green earth wire, ONLY from the bathroom water heater to earth. Check that it is connected and in good order. This sort of wiring set-up is waiting to kill someone. Buy and use only fibreglass framed ladders around the property because one day you will need to grab a ladder to clear passion fruit vines off a power wire and you do not want to be on a cheap alloy-framed ladder. Bamboo ladders must be reasonably safe too, but probably only when they are dry. The local electric authorities use them all the time in major installations and main road line repairs.

Decide now: Every home or building must have an RCD unit attached at the main switchboard before any power goes anywhere. RCD stands for Residual Current Device and they operate like a circuit breaker but operate VERY MUCH FASTER and save lives. Brand leaders in Thailand are Safetycut and Supercut but there are others. They look like a normal bank of circuit breakers but have two extra buttons marked "Run" and "Test" and a little turnable dial knob with numbers including "30" on it.

Safety between the road and your RCD switch panel. Whatever safety system is on the house switchboard, that power main wire between the road and the house with vines growing on it, is BEFORE your switchboard and the RCD on the switchboard in the house won't save you. Never trust anything electric here. Always wear rubber shoes as well as all normal precautions when doing anything electrical, and never use cheap alloy ladders around power in Thailand. You and that alloy ladder will be the shortest route to earth if anything shorts out! And you may well die as a result!

Medical, vaccinations hospitals accident and medical insurance. You need to have current medical insurance if you live here as there is no free health care like at home if you fall sick or have an accident. The local family doctor clinics here are for local people not Falangs, and for anything beyond a minor consultation everyone goes to a hospital. Any medical treatment you have except in an emergency will almost certainly be in a hospital, and the many better private hospitals here approach or match most overseas standards for most forms of treatment. The better private hospitals are certainly not "Third World".

As a non-Thai you will be treated and NOT be turned away from the local government hospitals, particularly in an emergency. Basic care is available but the rooms are not nice and some of the doctors will probably have lower qualifications than a private hospital.

Treatment will be free or inexpensive and many medicines very cheap. This is a huge topic and if you are young enough and without major health problems that would prevent you from getting health insurance then by all means you should get it. My health is good but my age makes the premiums dearer nearly every year. But research it well to make sure you get good value.

If you are to live near a larger city then you should/must go and have a check-up in a good private hospital there EVERY YEAR, and leave records with your name and contact details plus a copy of this check-up including blood type. Many hospitals have "promotion menus" of heath check plans in ascending price scales. Find a good one and return to the same hospital for a re-check-up every year including blood screens. If the hospital can issue you with a patient I.D. card with the hospital name on it, to keep in your wallet, then that is a great thing. If you arrive there in an emergency they know you!

If you will not be living near a big city hospital, it is even more important that you need to be sure you are in good health particularly if you are over forty-five or fifty. I recently had a full medical check-up in a very good private regional hospital for 3,900 baht plus a little extra, for a Stress EKG (electro cardiogram) test. If it takes more than an hour to get to a good hospital, like it does for us, a stroke or heart attack could very easily kill you before you get to any hospital, even the local government one.

You will need to be up to date on vaccinations for tetanus and a number of other conditions depending on which part of Thailand you are going to live in. Keep in mind that you now do not have a friendly local GP who knows you and emails you every year when your next PSA blood test is due. You will now have to diary all these things in your computer diary along with your female dog's next contraceptive injection and the next pest spray date for the mangos.

Snakes and venomous insects etc. Thailand has lots of snakes and most of them are not dangerous. Most snakes will move away if they see you first but some like the Malayan Pit Viper are small, quite pretty, very venomous and of uncertain temperament. Kraits are even smaller and also very venomous. We have seen several venomous snakes on the farm in the last few months including a luminous bright green viper. Some were in the laundry or garage! There are too many snakes to become an expert on, so simply treat all snakes as possibly dangerous and be careful walking in long grass, brushing under trees and turning over logs, rocks or sheets of timber etc. Folded tarpaulins etc anywhere should be taken by one or more corners and shaken out before carrying or handling. Venomous centipedes love that sort of hiding place too.

Do not automatically kill every snake you see but encourage them to move away with a long broom or bamboo stick. They may have a place in the ecology of your farm but not too near your house. Thai cats kill and eat small snakes very well. Keep a couple of cats at least. I found a dead small snake two days ago that our dogs had clearly killed judging by the size of the teeth marks. Always leave yourself room to manoeuvre when you are dealing with snakes. They can go from 0–60 in less than a second when they decide to move. Big snakes one meter and up can move REALLY fast. This may seem like useless information now but if someone is bitten attempt to kill and keep the snake to show the hospital so they can use the correct anti-venom drug. I mentioned dangers in handling firewood and sheets of timber etc. Always wear leather gloves. Not only are these prime places for snakes, but also for centipedes, scorpions and various biting ants.

Centipedes growing from tiny to 20–25 cm are venomous, common and fast-moving. They are flat with many pairs of legs sticking out from the body and are usually moving at high speed in a sinuous (snake-like) movement when you first see them. They are not to be confused with the very common millipede that is copper-brown and are round with many very tiny legs underneath, and rolls up when disturbed. They are slow-moving and harmless.

Scorpions are very commonly encountered under rotten logs etc and mostly sit in one place with their tail up to sting. Usually they are black and are reasonably lethargic but I have occasionally seen them move very fast. The black ones are up to about 5 inches long including tail, are common and have a painful, but not usually fatal sting. There is apparently also a creamy white variety that is even more venomous but I have never seen one here.

Red ants and Fire ants. Our property seems cursed with huge numbers of ants, although I think all of Thailand must be generously over-supplied with them. These two are among my pet hates – along with termites of course. **Red Ants (Mot Dang)** are about 1cm long and are usually seen marching in lines on branches or holding discussion groups on the ground around some dead insect or other morsel. They are very protective of their nests which are usually two or three tree leaves (live or dead) stuck together. You will get very good at spotting them after you have made the mistake of NOT BEING GOOD AT SPOTTING THEM a few times. The nests usually support a hundred or two hundred ants and are commonly associated with several other nests in the same tree. The ants forage in the tree and on the ground around their chosen tree and attack any animal or man approaching the nest area or tree. They attack fearlessly. They climb legs and brush off leaves onto hats etc and bite quite painfully, but the pain stops soon after the biting stops. The eggs of the common red ant (Mot Dang) are a delicacy in the North and North East where they are "farmed" for the eggs. Perhaps you will become a red ant farmer. Good luck to you on that! Each to his own! I hate them!

Fire Ants are also red but only about ½ a cm long and live in thousands in interconnected underground nests. These nests are to be recognized by small or large areas of excavated clay subsoil "grains" carried up and heaped up like sand around the entrance in circles from 30 cm up to a meter wide. When they bite it burns like fire and the pain can stay for hours, or a day or two for some folk. Stand in the wrong place for a few seconds too long sometimes and you can have five or ten biting your foot at once. Their nests also contain their "soldiers" who are about three or four times the size, shiny black and with really impressive jaws. They come out when disturbed, posturing and threatening, waving their jaws, whereas the workers just swarm out and bite. I imagine the soldiers have a painful bite but I have managed to avoid it so far. Whenever you see one red fire ant nest there is almost always more nearby. They colonize by runways which lead to new major holes sometimes up to 1 or 2 meters away, but with smaller associated holes every 20–50cms along the track between the originating nest and the new satellite nest. After a few days or weeks in any new main nest location, they develop satellite nests radiating out in clusters. Incidentally, the Thai word for termites is "**Bluock**" and ants are "**Mot**." Red is **Dang**"" and black is "**Darm**".

Dealing with ants and termites. A product range called Chaindrite is marketed in Thailand for controlling ants and termites. The white creamy liquid in white bottles is the most efficient killer I have found yet. It costs about 800 baht a litre and is diluted 1:60 in water. The actual chemical agent apparently was originally a South African ant and termite killer called Stedfast which was designed to keep termites out of building foundations. It is just devastating on almost all insects including small hornet and wasp nests too. Be ready to run like hell if the hornets work out where the spray jet is coming from, but hornets hit in the air with the spray (if you are good enough) tend to lose interest in looking for you and fall to the ground to die. The same compound is also available in white powder form and is very effective but not as economical to use as the liquid one, which is incredibly efficient but not exactly dirt cheap to use. But I love it!

An active fire ant nest looks like a dump of red or brown sand with tiny holes which lead down to the underground nest. In spraying a nest you first look around the nest for satellite trails to new holes and spray them first so you don't forget them. Then I spray around the perimeter of the sand heap, looking out for other evidence nearby, and then work in to the centre. I use a "half spray, half jet" setting on the nozzle to disturb and penetrate the sand dump and help uncover some holes down into the nest. Spray all over until the "sand" achieves the surface of a fresh cow pat and spray well down into any holes that appear. They lead right into the nest. Flick over any big leaves with the nozzle, as they usually have entrance holes under them. Also rake through the sprayed soil with the nozzle, while spraying, to make sure the spray has wet right through their excavated soil and down into the holes into the solid ground.

Next day they should look like flat clay with no holes. Seen a few days later, any visible holes, ants moving or surface granulation showing, means you will probably need to spray again. If in doubt drag your fingertips through the dry excavated soil heap a couple of times and wait a few seconds to see if any little red ants appear. In my experience with Chaindrite you will rarely ever have to spray again, but that is probably why it costs more.

If you are killing termites in or near a building, I suggest do not use anything except Chaindrite if you have it on hand. Such situations are too potentially serious to take chances with.

HomePro, Do Homes, Thai Watsadu and other places sell inexpensive (250 baht) yellow and blue plastic sprayers with 5 litre or 8 litre tanks. (The 8 litre one is best.) I keep one marked "ANTS" permanently ready for action on fire ants or termites. Note, Chaindrite as a brand name is also available in other products, for example, Chaindrite-1 which is a black/brown liquid and comes in tins of varying sizes. It seems to be based on creosote or a similar compound and is used for dipping or painting timber, stakes or bamboo to extend their life for a few months till the termites and borer eventually attack them.

Other brands of ant killer. Chaindrite is amazingly effective but in comparison to other available products it is much more expensive. This autumn has been a bad season for fire ants and in my attempts to get the best value for my baht I am trialling other ant killers which seem cheaper. My latest is Sevin 85 by BAYER. It is a white powder in a white 500 gram cellophane bag and you dissolve 20 grams for

20 litres. That is one gram in each litre of water which in addition to its cheaper buy price makes it very economical to use, but I have not finished my testing yet. Provisional results are that it seems to work quite well. It may be much cheaper to use than my favourite but maybe I have been spoiled with my success with the more expensive product. After a week or so later I am finding evidence of survival or re-colonization in a number of nests sprayed with it. This is almost unheard of in my use of Chaindrite, but if I was cost conscious, had plenty of time and did not have a big ant problem, I probably would be happy with it and the need to treat some nests more than once.

Unlike liquid Chaindrite, Sevin 85 which is a powder, and starts to settle out of suspension after an hour or two and if you have some premixed, you will need to shake it well before use each time. In the midst of these high level scientific studies (not), my wife has told me that she has been advised of two other brands of "cheap but really good" ant nest control chemicals including one liquid which should also stay in suspension better than a powder product. So it appears that this subject is a work in progress for the time being, as this paragraph is a last-minute addition to the book anyway. Publication date for this book is expected to be around New Year 2016, so maybe I will have some more results available in a few months, towards the end of the dry season (May 2016). If this subject is important to you as a farming gentleman, send me an email and I will advise you of any updates. Your comments on your experiences with ant control would be appreciated by me as between August and early December 2015 we seem to have a plague of new fire ant nests. In some places whole new nests are appearing within only a few meters of existing or treated nests. It takes some keeping up with.

Clothing for ant protection is described under clothing a few pages back.

There are many sizes and varieties of ants in Thailand, mostly black, several of which can and do bite but not usually with the regularity and ferocity of the two red varieties mentioned above.

I will deal with termites briefly as if I get started I will go on for pages! They have caused me so much grief! Chaindrite kills them beautifully but prevention is better than any cure. Firewood stacks, heaps of bamboo poles and anything paper or wood-related containing cellulose attracts termites. Be ruthless. No stacks of anything woody anywhere near any building. Burn all prunings ASAP and keep "one meter minimum" concrete paths around all buildings so you can see them before they get into the building. If you are building, use concrete, steel and fibre-cement products; NO WOOD. OK? Maybe we need wooden doorframes and doors but try to use genuine Thai hardwoods which are slightly termite resistant.

Be careful and watch for those telltale covered "muddy" runways they make when they are coming to eat your house!! At certain times of the year, termites swarm. This is at night after it rains and they fly in thousands. Thais call them "Malang Mau" (drunken flies) and they come to your outside house lights in hordes. In the North, North East and in Cambodia they set up light and water traps to attract and drown them and they eat them. In the morning they will have shed their wings and crawl around your yard in pairs, following one another, one male one female.

This is why some people have contracts for termite prevention, with a contractor spraying all their house cavities several times a year. Some of those mating pairs must find a new happy home in some wooden building sometimes. Very unlucky for the owner of that building. My family maintain that Malang Mau are not termites but everything I have read indicates that they are termites in the swarming breeding phase like bees do.

Flying stinging things. Hornets and various wasps called "Than" are common everywhere in the country, as are mud wasps which we used to call "mason bees" at home. The latter are forever building little mud nests with a paralysed bug entombed in each one with an egg on it. Most of the hornets are variations on the Asian paper nest wasp which have now colonized much of the world, building little upside-down umbrella nests under the eaves of houses. They are much less aggressive than the yellow and black German or European wasps we know overseas and usually have much smaller nests than the Euro wasps which in some cases build nests of the cubic meter and tonne specifications. But, you do not want to blunder into an Asian wasp nest. I have while pushing a lawnmower and it was a memorable event. At first and last light and at night they can usually be found all at home, a bit lethargic, and vulnerable if you bring enough firepower to apply, all at once. Approach quietly and be prepared to leave in a hurry. The big red hornets build a 1 meter pyramid on the ground which Thai people like as ornaments (without the hornets.) Find someone who wants it and go out for the day. Don't go near it yourself. They are scary!

Mosquitoes and Sandflies: Or "Yoong" and "Lien" as the Thais call them. The sandflies which bite, are truly tiny, as are the fruitflies (Malang Wee) which DON'T bite. As they buzz around your eyes you will not know which is which until they bite you, (then you know that they are Lien). Mosquitoes can carry malaria, dengue and Japanese encephalitis which are fortunately not a problem in our area. I have a normal reaction to mosquito bites, but I am allergic to Thai sandfly bites which come up in big welts on me. As sandflies and fruitflies target the eye area for moisture, I have had one or both eyes nearly closed on occasion from sandfly bites several times. Systems for minimizing sandfly attack were explained earlier under "Clothing".

Chapter 5

Shopping for supplies and understanding Thai engineering

<u>**Buying supplies for your property in Thailand can be entertaining or frustrating,**</u> depending on how tolerant is your sense of humour. Thai retail is frustrating. Don't get me wrong. Not everyone in Thai retail is incompetent, but it sure seems that way sometimes. I try to find good helpful people who are local to me and reward them with my repeated custom. Sometimes this cunning strategy even works! I was in retail back home for over twenty years, and I am shocked that frequently even the owners or managers of businesses sometimes cannot be bothered with me if they do not have (or do not think they have) what I want in stock. They frequently just seem to tell any lie that comes to mind to get me out of their shop if they can't find some alternative item to sell me Right Now! I have been told to go away because I asked for help and did not know exactly what I wanted. I have some shops on my "never return" list because they are so extremely unhelpful, rude and grasping. It does not occur to many of them that here is a guy who will always come back and spend money if he is looked after, helped and humoured.

The most useful item to take shopping with you in Thailand is a smartphone. You can either take a picture of the item at home broken and in situ and show them the picture, or turn on mobile data in the shop and search for the item under Google images. But even the pictures do not help sometimes. In one large local building supply centre I shop at, nothing is priced and they do not like people wandering around unattended. Staff will dog my heels everywhere I go. I show them the photo of the can of mildew resistant wood primer undercoat I buy from them every time. Three or four times now, and with a different employee each time, it is always the same answer: *Mai me!* (Not Have). I then have to walk each time to the place the cans were stacked last time and bring the can out. It is the same with a particular irrigation fitting that I buy in the same shop. I can take one in and show it to them. *Mai me,* (Not Have) they chorus. I have that one's part number in the notes section of my smartphone. In desperation I have to write that number down and insist that they look it up in the shop computer or march out the back where they do not want me to go and pick up bags of it out of the bin on the wall. And each time no red face, no embarrassment, no apology. Just a shrug of the shoulders. I can almost see them thinking, "Damned smart-ass Farang. He just wants to show me up". No I don't! I just want to buy something and they should be able to help me. That's their job.

Trying to buy Methylated Spirits the first time nearly drove me to drink it when I finally got it. It is called Methyl Alcohol here, but still no one understands what it is when I ask for it. I clean all sorts of things with "Meths". If water will not do the job, Meths is my next solvent of choice, then mineral turpentine. "Meths" leaves an oil free surface which is often important, particularly if you are cleaning something to glue it. It is also a somewhat safer fire starter than petrol. It does go "WOOF" but not as aggressively as petrol. I love diesel or old black plastic planter bags for fire starting.

Many common western gardening tools such as good spades, digging forks and even what we consider a normal wheelbarrow are simply not available here. Most Thai earthworks, landscaping and digging is done with a digging hoe. These all-purpose devices are a heavy duty version of the Western digging hoe (not to be confused with a push hoe or torpedo hoe.) The Thai digging hoe has a strong sharp heavy blade and they mount the blade FROM THE BOTTOM of a strong long handle with an upward facing wedge which seems really weird to me.

Saw Horses: you cannot buy them anywhere in Thailand to a Westerner they are essential. Thais just squat down and work on the ground. I made mine by googling "saw horse plans" and looking for a simpler than usual plan. It has 9 pieces of wood. Four legs, two braces for the end pairs of legs and three pieces 1m to 1.2m long for the top. The three are in an I-beam pattern with the top one a bit wider than the bottom one, or four bits cut out of the bottom one to get the legs at the right angle. The traditional plan has several complicated and compound angles and are quite a demanding woodwork project for the amateur.

Next time I would go to the local steel shop (they are everywhere) and choose 2 pieces of heavy "C" channel steel & get them to weld four pieces of 1"water pipe on each one for legs. Most steel shops have someone local they can get to do it or do it themselves. They will be quicker, cheaper and stronger than you can make yourself. They will probably undercoat them for you with metal primer.

Thai wheelbarrows are one of my pet Thai things to complain about. They are simply abysmal! With apologies to *Star Trek*, "They have wheelbarrows, Jim, but not as we know them". Even when they try to copy the Western wheelbarrow form, they get the proportions and balance wrong and almost always the materials are too thin to be strong enough for any form of reasonable use or service life. They are cheap at 800 to 1,800 baht (common price range), but the shortcomings are many and they are not even worth that money to anyone who has experience with Western wheelbarrows. In Asian wheelbarrow design they frequently reduce the size of the front wheel and position it further back, so it is UNDER the front of the barrow, not "out in front". This means that they are that much more difficult to "push over" shallow obstructions even with a pneumatic tyre. When this position of the front wheel is combined with rear legs that also are also slightly under the barrow and not splayed to the sides at all, it means the support triangle they stand on is too small for the height x width x length and they just fall over all the time. Usually with a full load. My "best" Thai wheelbarrow falls over at least once every single time I use it.

Many local wheelbarrows have solid rubber wheels on them which makes them Useless. They are exceedingly hard to push and defeat attempts to "ride over" even small pebbles. The frame tubing and sheet-metal trays are too light and bend or collapse with just dumping a rock or a stump into them. The wheel bearings are often a bad joke and welds rust and break easily. Trays bend and rust out in weeks or months and the barrow will NOT stand up on their own with anything slightly off centre. I saw one Chinese made copy of an American wheel barrow in a specialist American retail chain showroom in Pattaya with most of the geometry right but priced at over 5,000 baht and I baulked at the price. I have regretted it every day since then and that company no longer imports them. I should have bitten the bullet and bought it then. It had a thick laminated wooden frame and a heavy duty metal tray and its balance was nearly correct in the right circumstances.

The worst Thai wheelbarrow design has two hard rubber wheels under the front and an auto dumping feature. There is usually nothing to hold the tray down and it will auto-dump without any warning. "Grrrr!" Because the wheels are under the front, just lifting the back legs a few inches off the ground to clear grass or rocks is to enough to trigger the auto dumping feature and you have a barrow of wet concrete on your lawn!

I have been in stores of every Thai home improvement chain in big cities, even Bangkok, and some of the stores are as big as aircraft hangers. Digging spades of any type including drain spades are not available. What they think are spades are really shovels pressed out of flimsy panel steel, square mouth or round mouth, with long straight, or short D handles, at 120 to 275 baht. Of course, you cannot dig with them. They bend. Digging forks: Not available. Garden type forks are available but made of mild steel and are at similar prices to the shovels but try to dig with one and they bend. A chain called Do Homes at last visit stocked shovels and forks of the Camel Star brand. Made from heavier sheet steel, they resist bending and cracking a bit but they are not by any stretch of the imagination a spade. I did buy several forks of the same brand from them, also a bit heavier, and paid 50 baht each to have two pieces of 8 inch by 1 ½ inch angle iron welded, front and back, across the top of each one to stiffen the four tines. They are a bit heavy but you at least have something to put your foot on and they do mostly prevent the tines bending. I then gave two away to friends. I brought two Atlas brand, Australian-made spades (one digging and one ditching) back to Thailand after my last trip home, securely wrapped, in my checked baggage allowance. First time Thai customs have ever X-rayed my gear. They looked like a gun.

Chapter 6

Getting staff and seeking help

Permanent staff. If your land is big enough, permanent staff will be on your agenda. Your wife will not be able to do it all on her own and there is usually a limit to what her family can do to help, unless they are being paid (See Temporary staff below). We are unfortunately near a major industrial zone in our region and it is difficult to get farm staff as we cannot compete with factory wages. We have had permanent staff "temporarily" as described in the first half of the book. In some "poorer" parts of Thailand, where factory competition is not a big problem, experienced farm staff are easier to get and more likely to stay in the job.

We now have a local guy who comes by motor bike every day and we are confident that we will find the right person or couple for us eventually when we want to employ again and we have a new workers' house ready and waiting, but we are in no hurry. But it is really bizarre. We could not get anyone for 9 months and then as soon as we found a guy we have had numerous approaches for work. We have already had one disappointment. The next time we take on someone we will make sure they genuinely want the work and for the right reasons.

There are a couple of categories of people who usually know about people looking for jobs. Shopkeepers in any of the local shops, either Mom and Pop convenience shops, or building supply shops. They know who is not paying bills or needs credit because they have no work. They also know who is trustworthy or not. Also the two categories of elected councilmen, the Or Bor Tor and Poo Yai Bahn are in touch with a wide range of people on a daily basis and can be helpful. See below.

Temporary staff. Temporary staff mainly comes in two types. People you know and people you do not know. The people you know are family, friends, and neighbours etc. who help you out, with or without pay, sometimes without pay but on a reciprocal arrangement that you help them when they need it.

There are gangs of workers available, frequently Cambodian or Burmese, under primary contract to a large commercial sugar or cassava farmer and he moves them round his properties, planting, weeding and harvesting. They can be available in groups of five to twenty or more on a day-by-day basis. Usually they come with digging hoes and possibly power sprayers available. If you see a gang working a Cassava or sugar plantation somewhere, stop and ask for the foreman and get a phone number. Or ask your local Or Bor Tor or Poo Yai Bahn. They usually know everyone and most local things! These labour gangs work hard, fast and cheaply but you must ensure they understand your rules are about what they can take home or eat there. If you don't tell them they won't ask, and they will think they are getting paid cash plus all they can eat AND carry home.

These labour gangs usually prefer to all work together doing the same work at the same time. If you have two or three separate tasks they will all do one, then all change together to the next job. This is so no group gets "the hard job" while someone else gets "the easy job". So, they usually do not like to be split up into ones and small groups or doing different work from each other, except if there is spraying to be done on a different part of the farm. One or two will do that away from the others. They may know planting and harvesting cassava but most are not skilled on orchard work and will have no natural idea what you are trying to achieve. We toss rocks up against the trees to keep them away from mowers and they rake them out into the middle of the mowing lane despite being told not to. They all have sharp digging hoes and get fourteen people working while gossiping and you have a good recipe for more than a few cut irrigation tubes.

They work hard and enthusiastically, but you must have structured jobs and good supervision to take advantage of their energy. If you don't... expect the unexpected. You have been warned!

Seeking Online Help

Getting advice using *thaivisa.com*, Asia's largest "ex-pat" social media forum should be a great help to us but I have had mixed results using it. They have dedicated farming and organic forums but no matter how specifically we word our query, we get multiple unrelated, "troll" responses or just plain stupid comments for every **one** helpful answer. Many of these answers come from people who consider themselves "universal experts on all matters", and in many cases we are sure they are not even living in the country, but they just cannot resist "breaking into print". Expect them and learn to just ignore them. Good advice from genuine local experts is there too on occasions, but you need to experiment for yourself.

YouTube **is your friend** or your wife's or partner's second best friend (after you). Hundreds, if not thousands, of Thai language *YouTube* clips including government and commercially sponsored clips are on the net waiting for a Thai speaker to learn from, regarding practically every subject and crop imaginable.

Thai *YouTube* is an absolute fund of information for the Thai speaker and reader. It may be no good to you, but sit with your partner if necessary to help her get the habit of finding what she needs to know.

Other sources of information. The Thai Government agriculture departments and some local district councils (Ampurs) publish leaflets and booklets on various topics associated with farming, certain crops and farming subjects. The local Ampur (district) holds meetings occasionally to advise on topics like promotions on well drilling subsidies or local road improvement plans which could affect your access etc. A member of your family should try always to attend these meeting so you get to know these important things. Get to know your local Pu Yai Bahn and Or Bor Tor well or any other officer from the council who frequents your area. They can advise you (or your wife/partner) about local meetings or local events that may be important to you. The Pu Yai Bahn is your most easily available local official contact to keep in good with. He may be handy in signing or witnessing documents for you some time. My Pu Yai Bahn signs my six-monthly pension forms that confirm I am still alive. Note: The hierarchy in local politics and councils is not an exact copy of the West and in some cases there is no exact equivalent official term or position to explain the function of a person you find here.

Chapter 7

Building in Thailand. Farming in the "Land of Smiles"

Building and laying concrete in Thailand:
Ah, termites, wheelbarrows and building/concreting: Three of my six favourite "living in Thailand" hobby-horses. (Okay; add driving, preventitive maintenance, and corruption, as the other three.) But here we are talking about building and concreting.

Building in Thailand can be a nightmare. Firstly there are possibly no qualified builders anywhere in the country unless they qualified overseas. In the countryside (and in many towns) there are no building permits, no building inspectors and no one to check the job but you and the builder. And he might be a "cowboy", but you won't know for sure till he has finished

In our first twenty-one months we did a major re-model of the existing farmhouse, then built a staff house and another house that started off to be a staff house but turned into an investment renter. Most of the existing house had already survived thirty years so with not too much concrete cracking (see below) I felt justified in spending the money involved in upgrading it for our comfort. This particular rant does not cover the difficulties – no, impossibilities – I had in just getting them to lay 12mm plywood floors correctly. They had to do four rooms. The fourth room they did correctly ONLY because they got tired of being made to fix problems that were showing up already in the first three rooms. It is not a perfect result but perfection cannot be achieved with Thai plywood because it is full of voids. The most expensive and best looking stuff is painted black, stapled along the edges with tiny stationery staples to hold the edge laminates in place to make the sheet look good. But inside, voids everywhere, even worse than the cheaper grades!

You have probably seen cracked or crumbling concrete in Thailand and wondered how such things could occur. Well, with the systems, materials and tools they use it is virtually inevitable that the job must at least sometimes have quality issues. If you build, you absolutely must be on site before they do any major concrete pours so you can force upgrades to the boxing, re-enforcing and under-fill, and supervise the pours. In Thailand much concrete is mixed on site in big black plastic "baby baths". But it is not necessarily bad concrete. I have paid for hundreds of cubic meters of concrete to be mixed on site. The good was acceptable to excellent. The bad was abysmal and even today continues to erode with every thunderstorm.

Even when we paid for 7 cu/m of ready mixed concrete from what I believed to be one of the better suppliers, for 88 sqm of paths, it arrived incredibly wet and sloppy. I have never seen concrete so wet. A 4 meter section of 12 inch PVC pipe split down the middle was used to extend the reach of the concrete chute by leaning it over my wheelbarrow where the on-board metal chutes ran out of extension (it crushed my crappy Thai wheelbarrow). The truck that delivered it was rusty and broken-down, encrusted with concrete with large holes (dripping concrete) rusted through the concrete delivery chutes. The last ½ cubic meter or so was delivered into a big steel box the builder supplied and was carried in buckets to the ends of the paths. That is why it has to be sloppy, so it can be scooped out and carried in buckets or dragged by three people with digging hoes up the length of the paths like stationary conveyor belts. I kept seeing my builders grabbing chunks of coconut fibre and fist sized bits of timber out of the paths and it was only when we were an hour overtime on the concrete delivery and I was manning my collapsing wheelbarrow under the 12 inch PVC ½ pipe I saw this rubbish coming down the chute and I built up quite a stack beside me, fishing it out, as it came past. Why it was in my concrete is a good question.

The cowboy builders love to lay concrete on sand, or straight onto grass or weeds. Just yesterday I saw a brand new reinforced concrete road, half completed, that had been laid on an inch or two of sand. The sand was bleeding out from under the new slab which is now predisposed to fail because it is unsupported. This is just unbelievable and unforgivably bad practice. Organic soil with live matter growing on it is not stable enough to concrete over. That is why overseas they always dig away the live topsoil before concreting. The old tank stand and several open drains at our house had been laid some years ago that way. If the sand has anywhere to move, and water gets in, the sand will start to escape and the structure collapses. It did and it had. I poured and rammed many litres of crushed rock into cracks and cavities under these drains and one wall foundation which had cracked and collapsed, cracking two opposing walls of the shower room of our ablution block. I did this to stabilize and then re-concrete the drains and to support the foundations under that wall. We still have two cracked shower room walls but I now know why and will keep an eye on it. I have already had to ease the shower and toilet doors. The doors are hollow plastic with hollow plastic frames, concreted in. Repairs are next to impossible and hinges do not hold well in plastic. We found out the drains and foundations had been laid on sand and this is partly why we have poured the paths around the house for rainy season access paths AND also to keep the water away from the foundations and the house perimeter.

I am not sure of the full circumstances but it appears that a house belonging to a sister-in-law may well be a case in point of bad building foundations. It seems likely that it may have had its entire concrete base poured on sand or some other soft, loose, or uncompacted fill. Because, at some stage, something pretty definitely moved, because a water pipe or waste pipe leaked and then the fill started to soften as liquid drained into the fill under the concrete floors, The result was consistent with the way we know soft fill or sand will behave when wet. The sewers and drains under the house became unsupported and the problem compounded with more leaks.

Eventually this caused movements in the walls that supported the steel work holding up the heavy concrete tile roof. The house was about fifteen years old and this happened twice in little over a year. She had recently had the house completely re-roofed because the roof framework was collapsing. It was apparently thought that the roof framing had been built under-strength, but it seems that the problems were under the house base, not in the roof itself. The foundations under the internal walls must have been moving or sinking with the leaking water and soft fill because no sooner had they re-roofed it when the new roof started to fail again. Two new steel roof frames and two new tiled roofs in about fourteen months is something no-one wants to pay for. Her son, who is quite good with engineering and tools, managed to stabilize it all somehow but I stayed well away. I could not envy him that job. There were bags and bags of dirty fill that came out from under the house and were stacked up along the road beside the house for months until he eventually had them carted away and dumped. No matter what the original cause of the leak was, the fill and foundations should not have failed like that.

Thai cowboy builders will box on top of grass lawn or weeds, or virtually any surface, and they love to lay sand or soft clay fill, water it and pour concrete straight onto it. They also like the fact that filling the boxing with sand or clay will reduce the amount of concrete used. Driving into a local city several times over two or three weeks earlier this year I observed them boxing, filling and pouring concrete parking areas outside a new block of shop houses directly onto the existing weed surface with no excavation at all. Many (most?) Thai builders seem to have an aversion to hard fill. It probably scratches their feet when they are jumping on the reinforcing wire during the pour (see below).

Back to our 88sq/m of paths and 7cu/m of ready mixed concrete. This equals about an average of 80mm of concrete. They wanted to use 50–70mm and about 6 cu/m. The minimum in Western countries I am sure would be about 80–100mm. Unbelievably, in preparing the paths for concreting, they wheeled broken bricks, concrete, broken concrete blocks and tiles from right where the paths were to be laid, and took them 120m to dump them in an old watercourse out by the road and ordered in clay and laid it as a base for the pour. Unbelievable!

For this job they said they needed a truck of topsoil and I misunderstood that as they had started to box on the grass surface with no excavation. I hoped that they were going to use it to build up the land some meters out from the paths to allow for run off of water and to protect the edges of the paths. I asked if this was what they were going to use the topsoil for, through my wife who is Thai, and the answer was "YES!" Something obviously did not get translated properly.A day or so before the pour they start filling all the boxing in with the sticky clay that was the "topsoil" they had ordered, and I started panicking. "Don't worry. This is how we do it in Thailand," was the not-very-encouraging reply. It rained during the night before the big pour so I was up at six a.m. digging out 6–8 inches of squishy yellow clay and throwing in broken concrete from nearby where the clay came out. The builder came in at eight a.m. and reluctantly helped me. I smashed up more 3.75 inch concrete blocks to get more hard fill for the path, and yet they had wheeled ideal hard fill away to dump it! After all the work was completed I still found broken concrete rubble to dispose of that should have been a natural for hard fill in the paths, but they preferred to use clay or sand.

Re-enforcing. Domestic residence builders commonly use a very light gauge mesh with 8 inch (20c.m.) squares that comes in rolls. They roll it out, jump on it to make it sort-of-flat, cut it roughly to size and jump on it a bit more. They then add it as they pour the concrete and jump up and down in bare feet on it in the pour in an attempt to bury it somewhere in the 60–70mm slab. As it had various curves in it they usually fail to bury it all evenly and it is still visible today on the surface in odd places in the paths. In one place I noticed one of the staff hoeing away the fill on the outside edge next to the boxing. I asked what she was doing. She said she wanted the concrete to go down the edge next to the boxing there to hold the fill in. I rest my case.

After the boxing was stripped off the paths naked clay started bleeding out the sides from under the paths as I (and the female labourer) obviously expected and I had to poke around under the paths to find the air con drain pipes from upstairs, buried in the paths, and extend them so we can get the condensation water to run out of them. I then ordered in more builders mix, heaped it up against the paths and mixed and poured sand-cement and water slurry over the ramped builders mix next to 30-40 lineal meters or more of above ground paths which does a good, albeit ugly job of retaining things. That is until someone gets too close to it with a car or truck wheel, and then it cracks all over! Oh Lordy!

But wait. There is more. Because they frequently do not use concrete mixers, they mix concrete with digging hoes in big black plastic baby baths. With this system it is important to mix carefully and well and not overfill the tub. BUT, if they get tired or run out of time on a job they try to mix too much at once and get the proportions wrong too or have insufficient room to mix properly. You can get bits of concrete that don't hold together because the cement is over there and this bit is only wet sand and aggregate. We have two areas like that that still need repairing, but what are we repairing into?

Good and bad concrete. At the end of the day there is good concrete and bad concrete encountered everywhere in Thailand. Now that I have my eyes open, I notice sections of concrete on the roads and highways as well in brand new shopping centres that have only been open a few months where the concrete is already failing. From the finish completely vanishing from the slab leaving a noisy roughcast finish (most common on highways), to large unexpected cracks and serious failures along the edges of slab in mall carparks, a lot of concrete in Thailand appears to be failing prematurely. Projects of the scale of roads and mall carparks are almost never mixed by hand on site so the possible causes include site poor preparation, inadequate slab thickness, inadequate or inappropriate reinforcing and, of course, too little cement. The most obvious possibility is that poor quality cement, or (more likely) too little cement was used. As it is the most expensive of the four components in concrete, the most

105

obvious conclusion is that someone is making some extra money by skimping on it sometimes. Thailand is notorious for its corruption so always keep that possibility in mind. Where we pay separately for the materials and they make it on site, in my experience, they usually use too much rather than too little cement in hand mixed concrete. However, cement is valuable enough that if you are not watching, I suppose some bags of cement could be stolen off site by unscrupulous contractors and under-strength cement made, which will not fail until a few weeks or months after the builders have been paid and gone. There is no end to the number of things you need to keep an eye on when you are the site boss on your own building project.

Supervise, Supervise, Supervise. In short, you have to supervise everything your builders do. There are no standards and no guarantee of integrity of any kind. Everything is liable to be of variable quality. Our first three lots of builders were cowboys of one type or another. Our fourth builder has been great. We have almost no reservations about his quality. He admits his finishing detail is not his strong point and he gets other people to do that. I have still had to tidy up doors, window fittings and I am very disappointed with his standard of painting. To be fair he did get painting contactors to quote for painting our big investment house, but the quote was obviously padded and we did not trust them either. But, I am confident that nothing will leak or fall down. I would recommend him. You can give an unscrupulous builder specific instructions of exactly what you want done, they will agree on a price and then take every short cut they can think of to increase their profit, with no regard for job quality. I have even had builders just ignore everything I showed them to do and do it all their way, right in front of me, to my face as it were, as when laying my plywood over-floor.

Builders here all seem to want progress payments every few days and with a bad builder the guarantee finishes more or less the last day they are paid. There will be NO 10% retention of money as a guarantee on most jobs in Thailand. You have to watch, watch and watch everything they do like a hawk. You are a foreigner and you can afford to pay to fix it if it fails. It may look OK on completion but a few month later the cement may be bad and tiles will turn out to be poorly laid and "drummy" (having a hollow sound). I know I missed things but I picked up so many things. Some things like those concrete paths laid on grass were so extreme and so unexpected that they just caught me by surprise and stunned me by which time the concrete was ordered for next day.

Our first Thai builder just started ignoring the plans the moment my wife left the country. She got him to send her progress phone photos by LINE and stopped him by phone from overseas. We had to demolish the concrete kitchen benches he built when we got there because they were the wrong height and in the wrong places and rebuild them with the second builder to her plans (which the sacked builder had left on one of his wrong benches). The second group were a bunch of cowboys who built a wall with termite infested wood and laid the questionable paths. The third was a handyman totally out of his depth who we should not have asked to build a house for us. He actually laid out rectangular foundations eight by six meters with one side seven meter instead of eight. i.e. one side one meter shorter than the other. My wife and I knew something was wrong and in desperation measured the foundations before the concrete footings were poured. He eventually just stopped turning up. The fourth builder has been brilliant on construction with reservations about some of his finishing details, and of course the shortcuts his staff took with the painting.

So, the secret to building in Thailand? You need a good builder and that requires referrals or trustworthy testimonials from satisfied customers, and/or being able to see previous work and then the ability to recognize the difference between good and bad work yourself. It obviously helps a lot if you know a bit about building or you are at least, like me, a long-term, experienced "Do It Yourselfer", whose father was a civil engineer!

Chapter 8

Odds and ends about life in the "Land of Smiles"

Thai toilets: One of the great mysteries of South East Asia (so far as I am concerned) is the continued and in some parts, an almost universal use of squat toilets. Asians used to be less inclined to be overweight than they are today and are trained from an early age to squat for all sorts of reasons, not just the toilet. I can understand fit young people using squat toilets but for the several million aged, overweight or disabled Thai people this must be a daily imposition. Prices for basic non-flushing seated toilets start from within 200 to 300 baht of the price of a squatter. In Cambodia, Laos and Vietnam there could be more than ten million people disabled by age and infirmity plus the countless lower limb amputations from mine blasts since the Vietnam, Cambodian and Laos wars. And yet my predictions of a rapid transition away from squat toilets in South East Asia starting forty something years has never happened. Funny that!

Septic tanks: While we are on the subject of toilets: Most houses in the country, and many homes in the towns have what Falangs imagine is a septic tank, but it is not. A septic tank treats sewage with bacteria in a large sealed tank and distributes partly treated effluent around the property through what is called a field drain system. The Thai system is not a "septic tank system" but a "seepage tank system". It has unsealed tanks made of six to ten concrete rings stacked in holes in the ground. The rings have no concrete bottoms; four holes around each ring and an unsealed joint every vertical 30 cm (1 foot). The tanks receive toilet waste and allow it to seep into the ground in an uncontrolled fashion. Household "grey water" from kitchen, shower or laundry is usually separately directed into storm water drains or gardens. Flushing used toilet paper is banned in most Thai toilets because it blocks up the holes and cracks much sooner. That is why the little plastic basket or pedal bin is always to be found in Thai toilets, even today, in most hotels.

Of course this carries a risk (almost a certainty in fact) of ground pollution in the immediate area around the "seepage tanks". You do not want your neighbours (or even your own) sewage leaked at seven feet down, finding its way into the ground water system supplying the water to your homestead "shallow well" at 30 feet. It must happen sometimes, particularly if a new well is sunk near an old seepage tank or even worse, near an old piggery. When the tanks eventually clog up in twenty years or so, the man with the "honey truck" comes around every six week and sucks it out through a special hole in the top. **I thought you might want to know about** this piece of common sanitary engineering....... Or perhaps you would rather not have known! Sorry about that!

Transport fuels: NGV, Diesel and Ethanol.
In an attempt to cut down its expenditure of overseas funds on fuel, Thailand has embraced two aspects of technology to supplement its transport fuel supplies: Ethanol and Natural Gas.

Diesel starts life as a lesser refined fuel than petrol (gasoline) and is therefore cheaper than petrol (gasoline) to start with. This, plus its higher yield of kilometers per litre than petrol has given it a huge economic advantage as a transport fuel in Thailand. There are probably millions of diesel fuelled small vehicles in Thailand, most of them being pickup utility vehicles by Toyota, Isuzu, Ford, Nissan etc. Most of these are made or assembled in Thailand which is the ninth largest vehicle manufacturer in the world.

Diesel has two disadvantages, (1) pollution and (2) that the diesel or its parent crude oil, has mostly to be imported from overseas to start with. Modern diesel engines have steadily reduced their pollution levels but diesel technology seems to be is reaching its current limits as is signalled by the reasons behind the recent Volkswagen diesel emissions scandal.

The long-term alternative for most transport fuel in the world will eventually be electricity and hybrid petrol-electric cars are sold in Thailand in the luxury car market. Electricity is already a significant player in some countries for transport energy but Thailand will be need to wait to see further advances in batteries, fuel cells, quick recharging stations and hopefully, eventually cheap and pollution-free Nuclear Fusion electricity generation. Note: Nuclear fission in which atoms are split creates dangerous nuclear waste. Nuclear fusion which combines atoms will create no pollution. It is the holy grail of energy for the planet, if and when it is perfected. And I believe it is almost certainly "when", not "if".

Thailand does have large hydrocarbon resources but most is in the form of natural gas, not the crude oil from which petrol and diesel are most easily refined. Natural Gas is sold for transport fuel as Compressed Natural Gas, CNG or "NGV" as it is known here. CNG is low in common hydrocarbon pollutants, is cheap and it is locally extracted. It is, however, low in energy "kilometers per litre" even when highly compressed. Thus, it is mostly used in large trucks and a huge number have diesel engines that have been converted or originally supplied as suitable for locally sourced "NGV". The lack of "kilometers per litre" of NGV means that in a conventional car, replacing only the petrol tank with a gas cylinder results in very low kilometers per refill. **Taxis or any car running on NGV has to sacrifice luggage space** in the trunk or boot for a large NGV tank. Large trucks usually have from eight to twelve NGV tanks stacked in a steel cage behind the cab to replace the one or two compact diesel tanks they used to need.

Liquefied Petroleum Gas, LPG is available as a transport fuel here but it is not the same as NGV. The further refinement of natural gas to increase its calorific value into LPG adds to its price but its "kilometers per litre" advantages can no longer compete with NGV prices for the important price conscious mass Thai market.

This leaves cars needing an alternative fuel to petrol, diesel or NGV. As a major agriculture producer, Thailand is an efficient producer of grain and cellulose crops from which the ethanol form of alcohol can be distilled. Ethanol is not suitable as a 100% replacement for petrol in conventional automotive engines but can be mixed with petrol in a ratio of 10%–20%. Unfortunately it is highly corrosive to the conventional rubber seals and tubes in older engines and fuel systems. Vehicles made over the last decade or so use different rubber compositions for these sensitive parts. Even some two-stroke engines still contain standard rubber parts. We bought a famous brand Japanese brush cutter, new in 2014, only to have the fuel lines collapse in a few months and need replacing with ethanol resistant tubing. 95 Octane petrol without ethanol is still available at some petrol stations in most districts at a premium of 6 to 8 baht per litre. It is distinctive by being light green in colour. A hard core of people, mostly American ex-pats, refuse to use ethanol blend gasoline at all and there are some very strongly held opinions regarding the advantages of one type of petrol or "gasoline" over the other. Personally, I feel that it gives me better economy in my four-stroke Honda lawnmower than ethanol blend. That is my impression but it may be imagination.

Driving Licences: If it is appropriate to discuss motor fuels then it is probably appropriate to explain a bit about Thai driving licences. They are issued by the Department of Land Transport and the first licence is called a temporary licence and is valid for two years. Some people will tell you it is one year but they just don't realize the law changed in January 2015. You apply for each class separately and get a separate licence for each class. I have a car licence and a separate motorcycle licence. I now have "Permanent licences" as I have been through the temporary stage and mine are now valid for five years.

If you have an international driving permit and you are only here short term, then you do not need a Thai licence. If you decide to live here or are a regular two month or longer visitor, you can get a Thai licence by the fast track route where they issue a licence to convert your overseas licence to a Thai one. This absolves you from having to sit the written & oral tests that most of us would fail through language difficulties.

For each application they want copies of several pages of your passport, proof of genuine Thai residential address, usually in the form of a statutory declaration from your embassy, copies of your home licence or International driving permit (English language Ok). And a medical certificate stating that you do not suffer from an unusual series of five medical conditions that will surprise you:
1. Elephantiasis,
2. Leprosy,
3. Tertiary stage Syphilis,
4. Tuberculosis and
5. Drug addiction.
The full information is available on the net and many other books cover it in detail. Licences are issued to foreigners in a number of major cities, Bangkok, Pattaya and Chiang Mai etc but I only have experience in Bangkok. There, it is fully signposted in English and you deal with English speaking staff and you are prompted though the stages by computer screen prompts in English. The last thing before they issue the licence is a small battery of physical tests to confirm your status re:
1. Colour blindness,
2. Peripheral vision,
3. Reaction time, and
4. Depth perception.
The driving licence test criteria are currently changing and you would be wise to get up-to-date information before wasting time going there with incorrect documentation but in my opinion it is a very logical and non-intimidating procedure. They even have photocopy staff on hand to copy your documents quickly and cheaply. I remember that the licence costs about 200 baht a year, paid in 2 year or 5 year lots. Two licences for 5 years cost me a little over 1,000 baht.

Dog Ownership: Thais love owning dogs. In the countryside every house has dogs for security. We currently have seven dogs. In Thailand a "working dog" is the burglar alarm. Dogs sleep part of the day and their hearing is acute enough at night to wake to suspicious noises even when apparently asleep. Our dogs do a good job of warning us when prowlers are about, looking for stuff to steal.

Thais do not generally neuter or spay dogs but injections are available from veterinarians that last six months for female dogs and three months for female cats. But dogs in the area, male and female, all tend to howl at night when some local bitch comes into season and sometimes it is hard for human residents to sleep for seven to fourteen days or until the bitch finishes her oestrus. We have two female dogs, one spayed and one on the injection. They both join in the howling when a local female comes into season.

Dogs are fed a high ratio of cooked rice with their protein in Thailand and this seems strange to us. However, in the wild, lions and tigers tend to open and disembowel their larger prey and eat preferably or only the muscle and organs. Wild dogs over much of the world tend to eat the stomach and intestines, including intestinal contents and organs first and frequently kill again if game is plentiful, without bothering to eat the muscle meat. It also helps them avoid poisons if they are being targeted. Also note that in much of the West dogs are fed a healthy diet of "dog biscuits" exclusively, and they are formulated mainly from grain. So the Thai diet for dogs is not so different from nature or the dog food diet in the West. Cats and dogs have slightly different nutritional needs. Commercial cat food and dog food are usually slightly different in composition to reflect this fact.

In other countries dangerous feral or stray dogs are rounded up and if necessary put down. But here, feral dogs have become an absolute menace in some places but there is no official way of dealing with them. This apparently is because of the Buddhist prohibition on killing things. One of the most difficult things for Westerners to deal with is the Thai attitude to karma as it applies to stray or feral dogs, animal health, animal sickness and death. This doesn't get in the way of cooking a chicken dinner or a pork chop as long as someone else does the killing. According to my family you can eat meat that someone else has killed because the bad karma for killing it goes onto the killer's family not ours. This sounds a little precious to me because in Thailand meat is always available in markets and shops. Therefore no normal citizen is compelled to do a home-kill or hunt animals for the pot. There is always someone else to kill your meat for you and take the bad karma for you. Even more confusing is the fact that apparently very few veterinary surgeons in Thailand will put a dying or injured animal in pain "to sleep". It may not be against the Thai law but it is against Buddhist law. If you are an animal lover try to think ahead about how you will cope if placed in this situation. Stories are told of vets sending their entire staff home early so that no one witnesses the euthanasia. I point these things out for you as they are with no further comment. You can find links on *thaivisa.com* on this subject.

Home Security, burglary and theft: It is a nice thought that you could live in a gentle Buddhist country and not be robbed, conned, assaulted or burgled. But it is a dream. The truth is that people have all those security bars on their window and broken glass on the tops of walls for a good reason. Thailand is a country with few social safety nets and there are always people in need. Like in any country there are bad people around along with the good, and you must always think proactively about your own safety and possessions. Poverty, alcohol, drugs and greed are motivating factors in all countries.

You are probably no more likely or unlikely to become a victim of crime just because you are a foreigner. It will be just a question of time, place, need and bad luck along with opportunity (how easy you make it for them to steal from you). If you have a burglary or theft, remember your insurance will usually not pay out unless you can produce a police report to confirm that an offence happened and was reported.

At certain times of the year in rural areas people are out at night looking for roosting birds for food or walking home after a party or a wedding. In our area they walk along roads looking for frogs and certain insects after rain. This upsets the local dogs and disturbs peoples sleep. But not everyone out wandering at night is out to burgle you. But how do you know which is which? As they say, lock it up or lose it. But, sometimes there are localized spates of water pump thefts or fruit tree stripping just as the owner was about to pick the crop.

Our water pump was stolen two or three years ago and again in October 2015. We have had to install an upgraded steel enclosure to protect its replacement. Water pump and other farm thefts seem to move through areas in waves and in the worst cases they poison dogs a few nights earlier to make the theft easier. We and other members of our local family have had pumps and fruit stolen in the last three months. A near neighbour in a side road off ours had a dog die, apparently poisoned, a week after our pump was stolen and for a week or so there was lots of dog activity and barking at nights in our area.

Well, I am sorry to finish my book on a couple of "downer topics", animal euthanasia and rural theft, but this really is the end of my book material for now. For those to whom it may not be blindingly obvious, this is my first attempt at ever writing a book. Depending on the interest in our adventures, sales of the book and responses/comments received etc, there may be revisions of the existing information, additional material or highly possibly another book sometime in the future. Our personal situation is still unfolding here and most of the heavy work on updating the farm is over. It is now mainly maintenance, (water, fertilizer, pruning and spraying regimes), replacing trees and in-fill planting, and we have a full-time handyman employee.

So, now we do have the time to research ideas for developing the property into new and exciting areas. Currently under consideration are hydroponics, sprouts and salad greens in shade or plastic houses, melons, strawberries and even semi-organics. Thai-style organics focuses on clean water, natural pest control and minimal chemicals. It would not qualify for the organic label in the West but is a far cry from the way many things are grown here, too often with heavy chemical applications and scant regard for withholding harvest after spraying. The ideas that we decide are most interesting to us we will do pilot schemes on to test crop varieties suitable for our area, equipment and management methods. So, if this book is successful, there will almost certainly be a sequel and maybe even our own *YouTube* series. Any new book would include any information specifically asked for by readers and incorporate suggestions that could be usefully added to what I have already done.

You will note that I have not covered livestock (chicken or pig farming etc), care of buffalos or detailed management of rice paddy fields or specific advice to many other farming types. There are just too many farming types and I have refrained from offering advice in areas that are simply not my within my personal expertise. Yes, the people who choose to do orcharding will certainly get some extra specific help from this book. However, the general advice and background information contained in the book covers all aspects of farming in Thailand and remains appropriate to most circumstances. The advice on where to find specialized sources of local help, information and advice; family, neighbours, *YouTube*, your local Ampur, Department of Agriculture, your Or Bor Tor and Pu Yai Bahn etc, should also remain completely valid irrespective of your location in Thailand or farming type.

Thank you for buying and/or reading my book. If it is appropriate to your own current plans or dreams, then I hope you have found information in it that is useful to you. If you read it for other reasons then I trust that I at least provided you with some light entertainment if not a few laughs at our expense. Thank you again for giving the time to read it, and if you have not yet visited Thailand please do at least come and spend some time in our beautiful adopted country.

I can be reached at gordonbennettauthor@gmail.com. For reasons of privacy to protect my family situation here this is not my real name. I may not check this mail site every day but I will see your email and I welcome any comments that may positively add to my experience and thereby assist me in any further writing efforts. I will do my best to answer any reasonable questions received as promptly as possible.

Printed in Great Britain
by Amazon

37734306R00069